ADVENTURERS FE

ADVENTURERS FEN

Written and illustrated by

E.A.R. ENNION

WITH FOREWORDS BY
BRIAN VESEY-FITZGERALD
AND
JOHN HUMPHREYS

Colt Books
CAMBRIDGE

COLT BOOKS LTD
9 Clarendon Road
Cambridge CB2 2BH
tel: 01223 357047 fax: 01223 365866

This new edition first published by Colt Books in 1996

First published by Methuen & Co in 1942

ISBN 0 905899 41 5

Printed in Great Britain by Redwood Books, Trowbridge

TO
MY WIFE

ABOUT THE AUTHOR

ERIC ENNION was born on 7th June 1900 at Kettering in Northamptonshire, the son of a country doctor. From Caius College, Cambridge, he went on to St Mary's Hospital in London and joined his father in general practice at Burwell in Cambridgeshire in 1926. From childhood he was fascinated by birds and by drawing and painting them. Entirely self-taught, he sketched by observation and developed an uncanny skill in capturing their movements on paper. Some of his best examples were done during the daily round of his patients in the fens. He had three one-man exhibitions before the War and in 1942 published his first book, *Adventurers Fen. The British Bird, The Story of Migration* and several more soon followed, all illustrated with his own sketches.

In 1945 he became warden of the first Field Study Centre at Flatford Mill in Suffolk, where he ran courses on birds, insects, plants, freshwater ecology, among many other subjects, as well as painting, but left in 1950 to start his own bird observatory and Field Research Station at Monk's House on the Northumberland coast near Bamburgh, where over the next ten years he continued his courses, concentrating more on his first love, birds.

From 1961 he lived near Marlborough in Wiltshire, devoting himself to a prolific output of paintings for private commissions and galleries all over the country. With Robert Gilmor he started the Society of Wildlife Artists in 1964, and at the age of eighty was still sketching in Savernake Forest only four days before he died in March 1981.

FOREWORD

By Brian Vesey-Fitzgerald, F.L.S.,
Editor of "The Field"

This is the book of a man in love. And just as all the world loves a lover, so I am convinced will all the world (or at least that portion of it fortunate enough to secure a copy in these days of paper shortage) love this enchanting book.

Somebody once said that every great love story was a sad story. In one way this book is a sad book. For it is a memorial, the headstone over the grave of a part of Britain. Adventurers Fen is no more. The tractors and the grubber have done their work. Where but a short while ago the bittern nested is sugar beet. And that is the wages of war.

When I think of what was once Adventurers Fen and of what is there now, I feel some bitterness. And I do not know the fens well; indeed, I have only been to the fens two or three times in the nesting season. Dr. Ennion ·has known the fens all his life, and this particular fen, Adventurers Fen, has been his playground and his mistress, his spiritual and physical companion, for almost every day of his life. You might expect to find some bitterness in Dr. Ennion. There is none. I am not sure that that is not the most remarkable feature of this book.

I have said that I do not know the fens well. But I do know many of the birds that Dr. Ennion knows so intimately, albeit I see them in a different setting. I am not fortunate enough to have the bittern at my doorstep, I have never been lucky enough to see a yellowshank (though I have seen my rarities), not for me the courtship of the blacknecked grebe. But I have this in common with Dr. Ennion—birds and water, water and birds. They are the background of my home country just as they are of Dr. Ennion's. And I would ask no more of life than that they might always be so. In that measure can I understand Dr. Ennion's loss.

You will not need to read many pages of this book to realize that Dr. Ennion knows Adventurers Fen as it is given to few men to know their country. For to the blessing of a keen eye and great knowledge he brings a pleasant gift of language and a captivating brush. Many men can lay some claim to ability as naturalists, fewer to some ability as naturalists and writers of good prose, but those who are able as naturalists, as writers of good prose and as artists are indeed few.

Dr. Ennion's ability as an artist and as a naturalist, are confirmed many times. What of his writing? There is no outstanding merit of writing (as there are many outstanding pictures), there is no tremendous incident—though a yellowshank is incident enough for any naturalist in Britain. Dr. Ennion's prose is level—flat would be an uncomplimentary word—as level as the country he writes about, and he gets his effect unobtrusively, quietly. There is no out and out championship here, but the effect is even more telling than if there were. For Dr. Ennion's great quality is his sensitive intimacy with the ordinary and everyday sights and smells and sounds of his countryside. His book is warm, warm with the undemonstrative warmth of true affection: it is living, vital, homely. Yes, this is a homely book, homely in the sense that his observations are about our immemorial home, the land that has moulded our English mind. And Dr. Ennion is so benignly insinuating in his championship of his homeland that he made me homesick for something that is not my home, so that I had to go down and make quite sure no one was planting sugar beet on my mudflats, that no one was driving a concrete road through my marsh. Such is the power of Dr. Ennion's pen.

This is a book of small compass, with no great emotional range. But it is a book without one single discord in all its simple prose, unpretentious, true. It is, I am sure, going to find a permanent place in the literature of the fens.

And, maybe, Dr. Ennion is wrong about Adventurers Fen. The work of modern man has an air of impermanence, and once already has Adventurers Fen reclaimed its own.

B. V-F.

FOREWORD

To The 1996 Edition

By John Humphreys

IT was in the mid fifties that first I met him, an avuncular patriarch, a burly man with piercing blue eyes and a sunbrowned pate criss-crossed by scars of thorns, fringed by an old-testament halo of white hair. I was a schoolboy and a guest at Eric Ennion's Monks House bird observatory which crouched in the dunes of the Northumbrian coast, lit at night by the lighthouse on the Inner Farne Island. I was to return for many years thereafter, for the magic of the man and the place was compelling.

'The Doctor' as he was known was a man of immense talent but kindly and patient with those less gifted. Under his direction we caught, ringed and learned about the birds of that wild coastline. Even as a callow youth I recognised a man of exceptional talent and charisma; he was my hero. He came to Monks House from the Field Studies centre at Flatford Mill, but long before his distinguished career in conservation and painting his love of wild creatures and wild places struck root in the Fen country. This book tells of that time and place.

Eric Ennion was a GP in the village of Burwell, a man with as much passion for bird watching, duck shooting and rabbit catching as for tending his patients. The Fens were emerging from pre-war neglect and the final reduction of the marshes to farmland was about to take place. It was the last chapter in the story of fen drainage which began when the Dutchmen came over in 1760. Before the draglines rumbled in, the Doctor saw the last of it and with the keeper, Ernest Parr, he watched and sketched birds of the waterlands and drove his tiny car down the bumpy droves to folk in need of his professional services.

Adventurers Fen tells that story. It is an evocative record of the fens as they used to be, of the rigours of the life of a rural GP and a catalogue of encounters with birds, beasts and butterflies which have all but vanished from the acres wrested from the sway of the waters. This book is an affectionate obituary for a wild and beautiful place.

Brian Vesey-Fitzgerald described *Adventurers Fen* as "the book of a man in love". For certain, the gentle reflections of the author show a man at ease with the flat country, which some find disturbing, and its scents and sights now lost under the sugar beet. His illustrations are vivid and show a rare talent as a wildlife artist which was, even in his young days, blossoming. The author regrets the loss of his reed-girt marshes but without bitterness. His testament to "the glorious bird-haunted wastes of reed and water" is a lyrical record of the old fen, not as it is but as it was and maybe, dare we whisper, as it ought still to be.

I am proud to have been invited to write a new foreword to one of my favourite books.

JOHN HUMPHREYS

Bottisham, 1996

PREFACE

Iт is more than a year since the red and white surveyor's poles glinted above the reeds, blazing a trail for the draglines that were soon to follow. They came, each with a gaunt arm cutting the gentle skyline, clanking and threatening, laying their tracks as they rumbled along. They travelled on mats of heavy timber, picking the hindmost up by a ring, swinging it round and placing it ahead with the clumsy precision of circus elephants. Then they lurched forward a few paces on their caterpillar wheels and started groping behind again for the passed-over mats. Men cleared bushes and reeds away before them and dammed the water back in the ditches a section at a time. In a few short weeks the scoops had torn a channel twenty feet wide from end to end, ripping the backbone out of Adventurers Fen.

The water from the ditches and the interlines, the moisture from the peat, bled in an endless trickle into the deep new drain. It hurried, brown and swirling under a scum of broken reed roots, to and through a tunnel already laid below the lode by the western point of the fen: out of the bounds which had held it for heaven knows how many years.

When all was dry men set the fen on fire. Spurts of flame began to flicker here and there and presently leapt up to redden the fringes of the great smoke cloud which hung above them. An undergrowth of dried-out moss and litter nursed the flames along. Reed beds, sedges and sallows vanished in a whirl of flying ashes amid the crackle and the roar.

I went down afterwards. There was a single gull wheeling over the dead black land and a wild duck trying to hide in two inches of water at the bottom of a drain. A couple of tractors stood waiting to begin.

There is dignity in standing corn, a graciousness in the wide drills of potato fields starred with gold-spiked lilac bloom. But I regret the sacrifice of those glorious bird-haunted wastes of reed and water for the growing of sugar beet. No crop is less in sympathy with an English landscape than this alien. There are friendly gleams from the red and yellow mangolds, room to breathe between the rows and to set down your foot without constantly stubbing your toes. The fat purple shoulders of turnips squat goodnaturedly under crinkled leaves and there is a relish in their pungent smell. Both these were aliens once upon a time but beet has neither scent nor lustre. Partridges won't stay in it though they love to spend the day busking in the tilth and airy shade of a mangold field. But beet means work for many hands and sugar produced at home.

I wonder, when all has been tidied up and cropped, will I be able to find the exact whereabouts of incidents and rare bird memories? The lie of that cluster of rushes where I lay in the gun punt and watched blacknecked grebes courting less than a chain away; the site of the first bittern's nest in the county for close on a hundred years; the spot where a yellowshank, waif from America, stepped from behind a tussock and made me rub my eyes. They could be found, every one of them, under their shroud of fen wheat—even under the sugar beet's dull expanse of green—but I doubt if I'll try.

This book has been written instead. If it gives you half the pleasure to read that it gave me to write and illustrate, it will not have been published in vain.

There is a half-lie to confess: Adventurers Fen actually stretches *both* sides of the lode I have taken as my northern boundary. The fen lying to the north of the lode is smaller in area and has suffered a similar fate in spite of the fact that it belongs to the National Trust. The fen to the south has had a far more interesting career. It is an obvious unit and so perhaps I may be forgiven.

My thanks are due to many people; to the owners of *The Field*, the *Illustrated Sporting and Dramatic*, *The East Anglian Magazine* for permission to use excerpts from articles of mine printed in their pages from time to time; to the B.B.C. who have allowed me to retell part of this preface given in a recent talk; and, especially, to Brian Vesey-Fitzgerald, the Editor of *The Field*.

A countryman himself, his tweeds and pipe soon dispelled the unwonted surroundings of a London publishing house when I first ventured into his den. We talked of wading birds: he looked wistfully out of the windows, weaving a Hampshire estuary over the grimy roofs, and I forgot the discomfort of my best grey suit. Many a time since then I have had full measure of kindly encouragement. And now he is writing a Foreword for this book.

E. A. R. ENNION

Burwell, 1942

CONTENTS

ILLUSTRATIONS

INTRODUCTION

ADVENTURERS FEN lies to the south of its neighbour, Wicken Fen. They happen to be about the same size and shape but Wicken, National Trust Preserve, is famous: Adventurers is not. Wicken is one of the few tracts of fenland left undisturbed by cultivation—" a relic of primeval fen "— but in fact it has been profoundly modified by the drainage system round about.

It carries a dense growth of sedge. Because of the lack of water this is slowly being encroached upon by " carr," tall thickets, chiefly of hawthorn and buckthorn which need continual cutting back. It sounds absurd but a pond had to be dug there to attract wildfowl: the only other open water was that in the Lode and in a few ditches which were not secluded enough. Wicken, still full of interest, has lapsed from its virgin state.

Adventurers, on the other hand, was allowed to revert for at least ten years to a condition which must have been very like fifteenth century fen. Many kinds of wildfowl found and flocked to it.

Now, under a scheme fostered by war conditions, it is being reclaimed. The glimpse we had of what real fen was like will soon be forgotten. That is the motive behind this attempt to put it on record. It is never likely to get flooded for more than a short time again. The spaciousness, the sky above, remain but its life as an individual is finished.

My father settled in medical practice here in 1904. I followed him in 1926 and so have always had the fen at my front door. Its birds and plants and insects, my fellow countrymen, their stories, crafts and ways have been mine to explore since childhood. School, university, hospital, holidays, took me away but never for long enough to break the spell. And that, I hope, entitles me to write about it.

This tale of Adventurers Fen covers a period of forty years. Each decade has seen a change, and 1940 rings the curtain down. Up to 1900 the fen had been yielding its natural resources, turf, litter and reeds to generations of local villagers: these were the conditions I remember (as a boy) during the first ten-year period.

By 1910 the demand for natural products had almost ceased and a decade of agricultural activity began, later encouraged by the 1914—1919 war. 1920—1930 saw this decline and nature started to reassert herself. Since 1930 she has held unbridled sway—until to-day.

Adventurers Fen lies in a triangle made by the meeting of two lodes. A wide drain forms the base and some 400 acres are enclosed. The lodes, which carry water from the upland springs, run at a higher level than the water in the drain which comes from the fen itself. No one seems to know how long these waterways have existed in their present form.

The name derives from the " Adventurers " who launched a drainage scheme under charter of Charles the First. The Duke of Bedford was the ringleader and fetched men over from the Netherlands to show us what to do. Their memory survives in local place-names: New Gant (Ghent), Van Diemans and New Zealand (Zeeland).

But this triangle of fenland must have been known before their day. Surrounded by abbeys at Angelsea, Fordham and Spinney, close to Ely, it is more than likely that Bishop Morton, of Ely, tried to drain it as part of his scheme in the fifteenth century: and probably the Romans tried before him.

The lode on the south boundary leads to Reach, a hamlet huddled round its green. Reach was once the Water Gate of the Iceni, the port of the Icknield Way, and, later on, a city holding a famous Fair.

The north lode leads to Burwell. Stephen built a castle here to stop one Geoffery de Mandeville sallying from his fenland lair to burn and plunder left and right. Geoffery sacked Cambridge before he was caught. Pout Hall, the point where these two lodes meet at the apex of Adventurers Fen, must have seen many a strange ship pass.

These waterways did not run straight then as they do to-day. They were wide and wandered about the fens, but they carried the flow from the same chalk springs to the Wash and out to sea.

And long before that they helped to swell the Rhine of the Pleistocene as it ran through ancient forests on the North Sea bed. Then some continental subsidence split off Britain, made the North Sea and submerged what has now become that large alluvial tract fanning out westwards from the Wash.

Trees from the fringe of the forest still lie under the peat and not long ago a man brought me the lower half of a beaver's skull he had found while digging a ditch. The cutting edges of its great incisors were as sharp as if used yesterday. They had been buried about 2,000 years. *(Fig. 1.)*

Curiously enough, most of the trunks of these ancient forest trees lie in the same direction—their heads to the north-east—as if a terrific primeval gale had snapped them off and laid the whole lot low at once. This was certainly not fen country when the forest was at its prime, shall we say three thousand years ago? The tap-roots are in the gault—a stiff blue clay—and the trunks lie on top of this, two or three feet deep between it and the surface peat. The North Atlantic tides must have rolled in along the ancient valley of the Rhine and slowly washed the clay away from the surface roots. And then maybe, undermined and already tottering, the forest fell before the onslaught of some wild south-westerly gale.

What a crash there must have been!

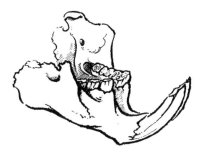

Fig. 1. Lower Jaw of Beaver

CHAPTER I

ADVENTURERS Fen was a grand place for a small boy as I first remember it. There was always something going on: a string of barges moving massively along the lode behind a tug, men loading turf, boys fishing. So much turf had been taken in the past that the general level was lower than in neighbouring fens. It was always plashy and mysterious brown pools spread below banks of meadowsweet and water mint. They were only old turf pits but looked bottomless enough to a small boy.

Two skeleton windmills did the drainage. They stood half a mile apart, each astride a narrow bricked sluice in which the slatted water-wheel turned when the wind was kind. There used to be more of them but these had been left to rot as the land they drained became stripped of its turf.

Ditches fed the central mill interline and the water, stepped from one section to the other, found its way into the Commissioner's Drain running across the base of the triangle of fen.

The high level system of lodes looked to the Great Ouse Catchment Board to keep locks and banks in repair. The low level ditches, inter-lines and drains belonged to the Commissioners: a body of local people who employed a fen reeve and men under him to " rode " ditches (trim away side-growth with scythes) and keep the interlines clean.

When the wider drains needed deepening the work was put out at so much a chain but the weed-cutting was done by the Commissioner's men. Broad knives fixed end to end in a jointed chain were dragged backwards and forwards across the bottom by two men hauling from either bank.

The Commissioners also employed a man to look after their engine at Upware which pumped the water by steam from the drain into the high level system. A lock prevented the water from running back and overfilling the lode. It spilled into the Cam close to the " No Hurry— Five Miles from Anywhere " Inn.

5

The Commissioners, to all intents and purposes, expired in 1940, taken over by the G.O.C.B.

With a few simple sluices at strategic points the old plan worked well enough. By setting the sluices the waterlevel could be controlled wherever turf was being dug: it had to be wet enough to cut smoothly but not too drowned to prevent the cutter seeing what he was at.

In a fen managed like this—wet, but not waterlogged—marsh plants throve amazingly; everything seemed to thicken to twice its normal size.

The welter of rushes and flowering marsh plants was called litter. Some was cut as a coarse hay for cattle but most of it died down to add its debris to a future layer of peat: small wonder that peat replaces itself by a foot every twenty years. The turf was cut during spring after the March winds had sped the mills and drained off surface water. It was stacked and left to dry all summer.

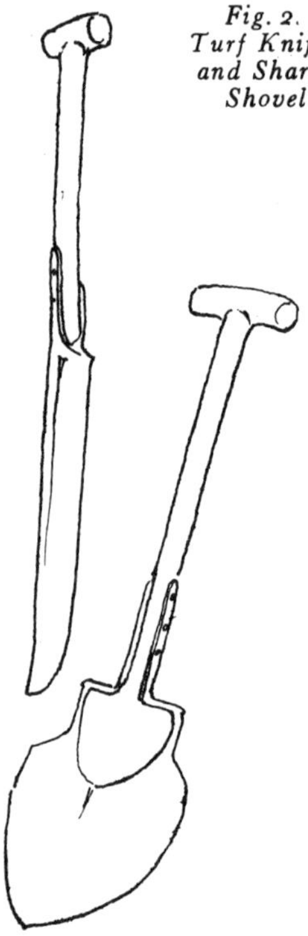

The turfcutter took four tools down with him; spade or sharp shovel *(Fig. 2)*, knife, becket *(Fig. 3)*, and an ordinary shovel.

Fig. 2.
Turf Knife
and Sharp
Shovel

Fig. 3.
Becket

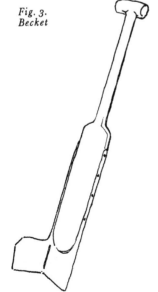

The spade, which had a forward cast, was shaped like an ace of spades but with two tongues rising from the blade to take the handle. These tongues were not straight like a garden spade's but bent, making shoulders to take the thrust of the cutter's boot. It was used to clear the surface waste and expose firm peat.

The rubbish was thrown aside with the shovel.

The knife, set on a shaft, was like a long butcher's cleaver. This made the starting-cut all down one side of the cleared strip and another short cut across one end of it.

6

Fig. 4.
Swallowtail
and " Cots "

The becket came next, gauging each slab of turf as it sliced and lifted it out. The becket looked rather like a thin cricket bat with an extra length of handle. The handle had a short T-piece grip, set over to the right a bit to give good purchase for the thumb and first two fingers of the left hand, since these had to guide each thrust. The tip was shod with an iron plate carrying a flange on one side bent forward at right angles. The becket was $5\frac{1}{2}$ inches wide (an older type 6 inches) and, allowing $\frac{1}{4}$ inch for the actual cuts, three turves came from every 16 inches width of peat. The flange was $4\frac{1}{2}$ inches deep and the becket-face about 18 inches long; it was not fully driven home. Both plate and flap were sharp and cut the back and one side of each turf. Its face and the other side being already free, the turf was easily dislodged and put aside by a twist of the becket.

The cutter, working from his starting cut, went down the strip making a trench three turves wide. At the end he turned back again and doubled the width of the trench by cutting another three turves, using the surface exposed on the way down as his starting-cut.

And so pits, six turves wide; one, two, even three beckets deep, made long parallel gashes across the fen. The waste was thrown back into the pits to help fill them up again.

Open walls of turf were built along the ridges in between to dry. The turves shrank as they dried and finally measured about 4 inches $\times$ 3 inches $\times$ 10 inches.

In autumn the turf boats, often towed by a donkey, came down the lode bringing planks, trestles and barrows.

A turf barrow had no sides. The bottom and tall front were of wooden staves—very like one

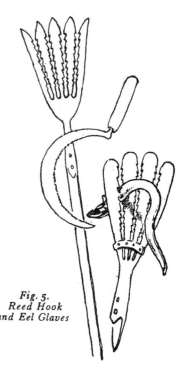

Fig. 5.
Reed Hook
and Eel Glaves

7

kind of porter's barrow but with a single broad wheel and more lightly built. Most of their journeying to and fro was done over planks set up on trestles to dodge the banks and ditches.

The wetter parts of Adventurers Fen grew a heavy crop of reeds. They were cut in winter after the frost had stripped them bare of flag. Young reeds mixed with the marsh plants growing among them would do very well for stacks: to thatch a cottage or barn they had to be tall and strong and clean.

It took about four years for them to mature. The aftermath which sprang up after cutting had to be slowly crowded out. The reeds themselves threw up hundreds of weakly shoots for a year or two and these were given time to die. The stronger stems survived and the bed was fit to cut.

Where the bottom was dry or glazed with ice they were often cut with a scythe: with a reed hook when growing in water. This was a short, strong sickle with a fine-toothed edge. *(Fig. 5.)*

A sheaf gathered under the arm was cut off close to the ground by drawing the hook across. Later the sheaves were laid together and armfuls lifted, shaken down, and tied in bundles. These were stacked by the side of the lode to be taken away in barges.

Litter was cut green in summer, later than meadow hay. The succulent stalks and grasses took longer to mature.

Sedge, a coarser growth, was cut in autumn. This was used in the cattle-yards for bedding and piled on sheds for a thatch. Cottages were often thatched with it too: the rough keeled leaves lasted even longer than reeds—40 or 50 years, if the thatcher knew his job.

One kind of sedge, sweet flag, was used to strew the floors of the monasteries and priories in earlier days.

Both litter and sedge were mowed by the scythe and brought home to the village by boat—low, flat-bottomed craft, wide in the beam and blunt-nosed. I well remember these litter boats moving slowly along the lode almost hidden under the huge piles they were bringing to the hythes.

There were osiers for wicker baskets, for eel traps and faggot bonds. The men kept their eyes on the willow trees as they went to work. A branch of the right weight and shape made a perfect stick for a scythe. This was cut and laid in the loft to season before being trimmed. Light, tough, never losing the inborn curves, it swelled with damp when used and gripped the iron fastening rings. During dinner hour scythes were kept out of the sun: the fittings might work loose if the stick got dry. They were laid in the ditch border or heaped with an armful of litter.

The docky baskets or frails which carried the dinners were platted from rushes. Another kind of rush, the real bulrush not the reedmace, was bought by the coopers. Its long round stems were placed dry between the barrel staves where they swelled with liquor and kept the joints watertight.

Men mowing in the litter kept a sharp look out for " cots," chrysalids of the swallowtail butterflies. *(Fig. 4.)* They hung upright on marsh parsley stems (the plant on which the catterpillar fed) or on nearby reeds. Each was fixed by a silk sling round the shoulder and by a hook caught in a tiny silk pad at the tail. The caterpillar spun its pad and girdle before it changed into a chrysalis.

There was a market for cots but many stayed in the cottages, stuck in the best teapot on the mantelshelf. They shared the honours with the sheaf of pokers and the reed warbler's nest in the corner of the front room.

In spring the men looked for plovers' eggs; in autumn, mushrooms, and on Sundays wandered along the lode sides with their darts.

These darts or eel glaves, made by the local blacksmith, had three to five barbed, double-edged blades splaying from a socketed base in which a long pole was fixed. The blades were often strengthened by a cross-bar riveted near the base. *(Fig. 5.)* The glave was jabbed about in the mud where eels were thought to be working. Every so often a lucky thrust caught one between the blades.

Stout Nonconformists all, who wouldn't do a stitch beyond feeding their animals, they nevertheless caught fish on Sundays. Is this an echo of monastic days? An oldtime entomologist saw a Camberwell Beauty sunning itself on the path before him but " Did not capture it, it being Sunday." He would have been allowed to fish.

The fen at this time held few birds. Snipe, peewits, redshanks nested among the tussocks on the drier ground: wild duck tried to bring their broods off in the reeds. Too many men and dogs were coming and going all the while. Reed buntings, sedge and reed warblers were the commonest little birds. There might have been two or three pairs apiece

9

of grasshopper warblers, whitethroats, linnets, meadow pipits *(Fig. 6)*, larks and yellow wagtails.

It was the insects that really attracted me then—the big brown dragonflies, the peacocks and red admirals in July besieging the pink clusters of hemp agrimony. A few tattered swallowtails kept them company: they emerged in May, with a small second batch in September.

Fig. 6. Meadow Pipit

Best of all were the big caterpillars; drinkers, emperor, elephant hawk on the litter; puss and eyed hawk on the low-growing sallows just at the right height for a small boy to find. My eyes were sharp and I must have found and reared scores of elephant and eyed hawk caterpillars. The skin of the elephant was smooth as mole-brown velvet, etched with a network of fine creases *(Fig. 7)*: it had big shaded " eyes " on its snout. Some of these disappeared when the elephant shrank with fright to reappear little by little as the beast regained confidence. That taught me to beware of Nature books: they said it would suddenly show its eyes to startle its enemies. Mine did the opposite.

The freckled green form of this caterpillar was uncommon but the two phases of the eyed hawk—one the blue of frosted grass, the other greengage green—turned up in equal numbers.

I still stop at the stripped shoots of a sallow bush to find the culprit. *(Fig. 8.)* The caterpillar, stout and rough as shark's skin, grips the stem with its claspers and last two pairs of (pro-) legs. The (true) front legs press tightly towards the pointed apex of the head, making the outline of a sallow leaf from whichever way you look.

Fig. 7. *Elephant Hawk Caterpillar*

They burrowed and turned to chrysalids in my box of peat: next May the moths came out.

An eyed hawk in a cabinet is a lovely but lifeless thing. Fresh from the chrysalis, hanging taut-winged with body proudly curling up it is far lovelier, even though the flushed eyed under-wings are overlapped. *(Fig. 9.)*

The elephant hawk with its pink and olive shading was just as beautiful when it clung to my sleeve by its new white legs. I know now that it was the looking forward to seeing this loveliness of newborn curve and pattern that made me hoard chrysalids like gold through the winter months.

A few of each kind were killed for a collection, the rest set free.

Fig. 8. *Eyed Hawk Caterpillar*

Fig. 9. *Eyed Hawk Moth*

CHAPTER II

THE demand for turf fell year by year. New houses sprang up in the villages, old cottages were modernized but the stoves and fireplaces put in were never meant for peat. This wanted an open hearth to burn on, glowing red all day and smouldering all night. There were fires in the village which hadn't been out for years.

The old hearths with their jacks and beams and echoing chimneys—looking up you saw a big square hole of sky—were all bricked-in, leaving just room enough for a kitchen range. Years before many of them had been partly filled with Victorian hobgrates, in some cases coupled with the facing of the house itself with brick. These bricks, a sickly yellow-white, were made from local clay. How the founder of the brickyard must have beamed to see the main street of his village thus transformed.

The bright clunch-built walls a yard thick at the back of the houses are still there: the village looks its best from the narrow backways.

The blacksmith remained one of the fen's few customers. He used turf to heat the iron cartwheel tyres. Turves were set up in pairs all round the tyre and lit. When they had burned themselves out the wheel was fitted inside the red-hot tyre and this was hammered into place. Buckets of water cooled it down and, as it cooled, it shrank and gripped the rim. The sizzling clouds of steam and acrid smoke outside the smithy; I can see and smell them yet.

The new roofs carried slates instead of thatch or mellow tiles. When the reed or sedge thatch of old houses needed mending it got botched with handier wheatstraw and even covered up with sheets of corrugated iron. The reedbeds stood unwanted in the fen and no one cut the sedge.

But for all that there was more activity there of a different kind than ever before. The new aim was not to control the water but to banish it. Dry the fen, plough in the sedge, plough deep and marry clay with peat to lighten the one and stop the other blowing away: grow wheat, twenty-one comb to the acre, barley, mustard and beet.

Some of the fields were pipe-drained: lines of earthenware pipes buried in trenches all leading into a ditch. Some were turf-drained: long strips of topsoil removed to expose the underlying gault. Gutters were dug along this, filled with turf and the topsoil put back. A special becket four inches wide was used to cut the turves.

It was the old, old cry: is not a fat sheep better than a goose, a stalled ox better than a dish of eels? That's what the Adventurers said in 1630, but the Bailiff of Bedford (the floods from the Bedfordshire watershed) came down and they failed. He was yet to come again.

The new adventurers deepened the ditches and furbished up the nearer mill. They didn't worry about the other one, it was too far off and left to tumble down. They didn't worry about the far end of the fen at all, it was such a long way from the high road and their farms. A few young horses were turned in to graze.

Transport became a curious problem. The lodes were close to hand with barges in them slowly rotting away. The droves, ample for the light traffic of earlier days, ran straight and green. Harrows used to be run over them in spring to level the winter's ruts. They were wide enough to take four lines of traffic abreast but cart after cart went blindly follow-my-leader down a single track. *(Fig. 10.)*

No one could spare an hour for harrowing: the wheels scored deeper and deeper every day. After autumn rain it was not unusual to see three straining horses pulling one load of beet through mud spread in a level sticky pudding up to the axeltree. And beet grown within a stone's-throw of the river bank being carted five miles to railhead at that. Even with the increased traffic and the tractors a spread-over-land-and-water policy might have done much to ease the transport problem. Man was ever too anxious to get there before his neighbour so they clamoured for new roads while the barges quietly sank.

But this didn't bother a schoolboy back on his holidays. Three half-sunk barges lying nose to stern beside the bank were a godsend to me. The first was well down by the bows, the second waterlogged, the third had its cabin high and dry, a refuge during storms.

This was the stronghold of a school of chub as well as of a schoolboy. Some of them must have scaled between three and four pounds. Every boy is a fisherman at heart. Those who have the patience to sit watching a float for hours become real fishermen. The others—and I was one of them—don't, but they can't resist watching fish.

All days began by fishing from the bank. Sooner or later, according to what luck, they ended on the barge, lying full-stretch along the blistered planks dangling a short line overboard for chub.

Fig. 10.
" *Three horses pulling one load of beet* "

I never caught one.

They came weaving through the tall green waterweeds, nose down, sucking at the bottom round the bait. *(Fig. 11.)* They sniffed at it, stirred it disdainfully with lazy tails and slid back to the shadow of the barges.

Every so often with the rhythm born in every natural creature round they came again, found a fresh bait and swam away. I had all the bigger ones by heart, either by slight differences in shape or by the patches of white fungus on their scales.

Bream were the commonest fish in the lodes, dull, flat, slimy things. A hole was baited in the evening and the experts returned to start fishing before dawn. Sometimes they fished all night with a bit of white paper fastened to the float. The catch was reckoned by the stone and carried home in sacks.

They caught tench too, dark golden-green with leathery skins and sleepy eyes, and perch and red-finned roach and eels.

I was allowed to go down fishing all night too. I could swim and summer nights are never very dark.

The lode lay very still and black. There was no lapping at the barges. The little shivery winds that spring from nowhere and as suddenly depart made no stir on the surface. The only break would be the spinning of a moth fallen in and whirring to take off.

Sedge warblers chittered intermittently all night and rustled by the banks. Waterhens croaked and watervoles dived in with startled plops. You could hear the faint rasp as they ate the pulpy rush stalks and imagine them sitting up, supper in forepaws, on their rafts.

Wisps of mist came curling down the lode and, as dawn spread, the fen woke under a thick blanket that grew whiter every minute. The sun had risen well above the willows before the last remnants fled.

The north-east corner of the fen was soon under cultivation. It lay a trifle higher than the rest. The southern corner was lower and less well placed for drainage. It was deeply furrowed with old turf diggings always half-full of water. Much of it never advanced beyond rough grazing ground.

The rest was brought round by digging still deeper ditches and by cutting a ten foot drain half a mile long for them to empty into. It finished close to the Commissioner's Drain on the eastern boundary. A pump, driven by a tractor, sent the water down a shallow wooden trough across the space between.

Even so, this land was never much good for wheat. The black soil was too light to cake: the drier it got the more powdery the tilth. Dust devils whirled across on every sunny day. Much of it blew away because they didn't plough deep enough to find the clay to bind with it: it looked so fertile wet and newly won that their one obsession was to get it sown.

Wheat thrives amazingly on new fen soil for the first few years, but unless the plant can be firmly bedded down by rolling, half the yield is spoiled. Dry peat won't roll.

The tall top-heavy stalks got knocked about by wind and rain. A patch was battered down, a gap in the defences; the standing wheat beyond couldn't bear the strain and so the mischief spread across the field. Rank fen bindweed clamped it down, broods of wild duck on their nightly forays pattered round and undermined the edges with their runways. The corn by the borders of the field generally stood since it was protected by the reeds and hemlocks of the ditches.

Laid wheat does not get enough air and sunshine to harden and ripen the grain. It is difficult to cut, though the high yield of the part that can be harvested in good condition helps to offset the bad. There may be a bumper crop in a lucky season but it's safer to turn up the clay.

Some heavy crops of sugar beet and potatoes were gathered and then, for a change, they started growing bulbs. Once again this English fenland was beholden to the Dutch.

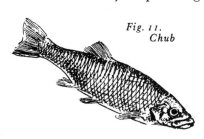

Fig. 11.
Chub

The cottage at New Zealand by the Reach lode bank, built there a hundred years before, was tidied up and another placed alongside. The sheds were overshadowed by a big new barn of brick and concrete pillars. They roofed the cottages with slate; the barn at least was thatched, rather clumsily, with reeds and sedge.

Mill Road, an ancient right of way across the fen, was straightened, raised and widened. A slatted bridge crossed the new ten foot drain. Some poplar trees were planted near it and variegated hollies (heaven knows why) set hopefully along another remade track closer to the cottages. Perhaps the farmer had a brother in the wreaths and crosses trade: Holly Tree Road did not survive the bleak fen winters.

These new roads and buildings meant little to me. Bulbs and hollies were a pleasant innovation; the rest had been seen in neighbouring fens a hundred times before. The change, of course, wiped out the old fen plants and fauna. Weeds and birds, corn buntings, larks and partridges from the fields around, moved in. But a flood upset the applecart again in 1920.

The neglected western point of Adventurers Fen was far more interesting. Beyond the bustle of New Zealand the bank led past a line of trees and away for a mile to Pout Hall.

Fifty years ago a cottage stood here on the opposite bank of the lode. It was derelict then and slowly settling down. Nothing remains to-day but a few ragged fruit trees and the name.

" Hall " is often found in fenland applied to a cottage or small farm, many of them in little better condition than Pout Hall. Tenants had to saw bits off the legs of furniture to make them fit the floors. Walls, ceilings, even the great chimney breasts leaned at alarming angles. It was a test of agility to climb upstairs.

" Hall " was no flight of fancy on the owner's part. It meant " a roof over your head " to Danes and Saxons, and to the fenland Celts both came to plunder. Sites to build on in the fens were few and far between. New houses rose from the ashes of the old and, as happens still, retained the name.

I turned off between the trees along the roadway leading to the forgotten mill. It was overgrown with reeds and sallows and best followed by the feel of hard ground underfoot as against the spring of peat on either side. The wide ditch running by it was half-choked too and so was the interline beyond. They made in effect two chains of narrow sheltered pools, meeting at the mill. The mill at the crossing, now almost tumbled down, was a good observation post.

Duck which hitherto had only used the fen for breeding stayed the year round. Mallard and teal feathers, plucked while preening, drifted on many of the little pools. There were no open spaces for peewits and redshanks: water rails squealed and grunted in the tangled growth instead.

There had always been a few low mounds, unseen above the sedges, with bushes growing on them. Already the thorns had grown dense enough to harbour a pair of jays and a little owl.

The ground seemed sodden but the pull of distant drainage was being felt. Sapling buckthorn, hawthorn and guelder were springing up everywhere—the beginning of carr-growth. Blackbirds, linnets, turtle doves, whitethroats, wrens and tits were in possession and I found a lappet caterpillar sprawling on a bush.

This land was later acquired by the National Trust. Like Wicken Fen itself it was a splendid hunting ground for moths. These were taken by setting up a big white sheet lit with the beam of an acetylene lamp, and by smearing patches of treacle on the tree trunks and posts. A net and a supply of pill-boxes were wanted too.

It was an experience to see the main drove on Wicken Sedge Fen with half a dozen sheets lit up along it. The more moist and overcast the night the better: moths like damp, and the white sheet spread its influence farthest on a dark night. A sky growling and flickering with imminent thunderstorm was often excellent. But whether or not the collector got the moth he wanted depended largely on the season. The date of emergence varied from year to year for the different species. If the moth was " out " a good night increased the chances: neither treacle nor light could attract a chrysalis.

Lappets, drinkers, poplars, privets came crashing at the sheet to cling and quiver for a moment before swirling back into the night. Ermines, wainscots, prominents (which seldom arrived until after midnight) and a host of lesser fry flashed in and out of the light.

Sometimes one particular moth, known perhaps by a slit in its wing, came again and again. The only remedy was to catch it and put it in a box to sober down.

Each kind behaved in a way of its own on arrival. Some touched and were gone, some careered madly round and round the lamp, some hit the sheet, folded their wings and promptly went to sleep. Some dropped at once and lay still in the folds at the foot, some were found sitting tight on the back of the sheet. There was little need to examine a moth to know what sort it was.

And so at the treacle patches: a beam from a torch was slid on cautiously and the net held ready. Some kinds skipped away at the first hint of danger, some fell off into the grass, where it wasn't easy to find them, and some wanted flicking off. A wanted moth was taken from the patch by picking it off with a pill-box—a trick that needs practice to do skilfully with one hand. Thumb and forefinger hold the lid " hinged open " above the box, which is held by the other fingers against the palm —just widely enough to take the moth and gently enclose it as the lid comes down.

Flies, earwigs and stray wasps came to treacle too. Centipedes and snails climbed up the posts for their share of the sweets. Spiders waited under the table to haul off late revellers.

Most moths stopped flying soon after midnight but there was often a short, sometimes very productive, flight just before dawn. It was not worth going to sleep betweenwhiles though men sat nodding at the empty sheet and the treacle rounds became more and more infrequent.

Mosquitos, forgotten in the excitement of the earlier hours, bit with vigour and persistence. Their din never ceased and the steady wheezing of baby shorteared owls across the fen was almost as maddening. Nevertheless don't miss Wicken on a damp June night if you get an invitation.

Fig. 12. Blacktailed Goduit

CHAPTER III

A FELLOW undergraduate and I were lying on a litter stack watching a godwit through our glasses. This was in March 1928, and the stack one of twenty standing along the eastern boundary of Adventurers Fen between the head of the new drain and Burwell lode bank. Another line of them lay beside the lode: perhaps fifty in all, litter or mustard straw, rotting half-buried in nettles and bindweed. Litter during the Great War years had fetched the price of good meadow hay: now it was worthless and not being cut any more.

(*Fig. 12.*) The godwit was feeding in a pool with half a dozen redshanks, some peewits, gulls and a number of small shore waders—ring plovers and dunlins. The pool lapped at the foot of our stack. It was one of many on what might well have been the floor of an estuary uncovered at low tide. But the mud was black and sprinkled with the sprouting tops of last year's sugar beet. A row of furrows down one side of the field showed where ploughing had started before the soil got too wet.

Fig. 13.
Corn Bunting

Fig. 14.
Whinchat

The godwit whistled a warning and flew away. The other birds stopped feeding and waited with uplifted heads. They moved off and settled farther down the pool.

A workman passed behind us with a couple of petrol tins slung round his neck. Presently there was a splutter from the tractor beside the pump. Day after day the tractor chugged away and the water slowly vanished. The birds went too.

They carted a good crop of mustard off that field but the extra cost involved in draining and waiting while bogged tractors were dug out must have halved the profits. Each year less land was being ploughed and weeds and grasses spread unhindered. The wilderness was advancing cautiously against the cultivated soil. When you " don't get nuthin' for the stuff an' pay a boy a man's wages " it was not to be wondered at. Nevertheless for a while they grumbled and struggled on. The Bank took over New Zealand and put an overseer in.

It's not for laymen to criticize agricultural policy but they may put down what they see. Certainly these fen farmers had made money from their hasty reclaiming of fen land during the past ten years. The price obtained for whatever they produced was not under their control. The price held for every one alike wherever they farmed. How much of it became profit depended partly on foresight in putting some of it back into the land by way of improvements and manure and partly, of course, on the skill and economy with which a farm was run. Little enough went back into Adventurers Fen : perhaps there wasn't much surplus to spare.

The drainage rates stood at about £1 an acre—with no guarantee against flooding. Sometimes for weeks at a stretch it was impossible to get on the land at all. Time was wasted on the miles of bad road between work and farm buildings, in cutting laid corn, in digging-out bogged tractors and oaks. Oaks were trunks of fallen timber lying on the gault under the peat. They were not all oak ; alder and yew were found as well. These were the remains of ancient forests and had to be split and hauled aside before ploughing could go on again. The wood was useless for carpentry ; it shivered to bits as it dried.

In windy springs the whole first sowing of beet was often lost—blown away with the top layer of soil to be piled in the headland ditch. Sometimes a second sowing followed suit. Heavy yields were needed to compensate for all this and the gilt of virgin soil was already beginning to wear thin.

Every year, because of neglected ditches, the winter flood water took longer to drain away. Cleaning had to be scamped to get seed in before it was too late. Harvests, always behind in the fens, were later yet and spoiled by autumn gales and rain. Shocks standing at Christmas were not unknown and many a sheaf lay sprouting green on the sodden ground. There was a temptation to sow late crops in the handiest fields and leave the rest. A field left idle for two years could be counted out: it would need ploughing twice and half a dozen harrowings to bring it back. No one had the heart to tackle that.

By 1930 the only arable land was a block of less than a hundred acres in the north-east corner. All the rest became a testing ground between two rivalries, summer heat and winter flood. It was a very pleasant wilderness for a naturalist to wander in either way, although the conditions were by no means those of virgin fen. Flooding reached its maximum in April, drought by mid-July. Except at the western end there was as yet no widespread growth of reed or sedge.

The reeds (PHRAGMITES) grew in long double lines beside the ditches, where they had always grown: sedges (CLADIUM and CAREX) and flags (IRIS) apeared in patches here and there. The reedmaces (TYPHA), bur-reed (SPARGANIUM) and the larger rushes (SCIRPUS—the true bulrush—PHALARIS and GLYCERIA) grew mainly along the borders of the interlines where their roots had been least disturbed. The roadways and the ridges between turf pits formed the chief beds of the smaller rushes (JUNCUS). These did not take kindly to immersion and nearly everywhere else was covered at least a foot deep in flood time.

The common weeds brought in by cultivation soon died. True water-weeds, found in the ditches, had barely begun to creep out.

In spite of all the ploughing, harrowing and harvesting, the seeds of countless marsh plants must have lain dormant in the peat. No sooner did the water begin to dry off in summer than the fen became carpeted once more: all the marsh varieties of mint, orchid, bedstraw, vetch, thistle, parsley, comfrey, willowherb, loosestrife and many more sprang into life as if they had never been upset. They didn't grow with the vigour seen in litter but were all the easier to appreciate for that.

This revival was best seen in the fields to the south of the mill. They were as green as you please though the ridge and furrow of ploughing could still be felt underfoot. The mat of short field grasses was varied by

Fig. 15. Stonechat.

great waves of taller kinds. Rush tussocks, banks of meadowsweet and agrimony vied with the statelier single growth of marsh thistles and angelica. All bore the grey watermark of recent flooding for a handsbreadth up their stems.

Marsh parsley became plentiful enough to bring back the swallowtails; they breed here again for several years. Ruby tigers, plusias and crowds of butterflies danced over the sunlit flowers: the rare little Essex skipper left its knapweed on the droves to join them.

In August there were puss, pebble and pale prominent caterpillars on the sallows. Poplar hawks, kittens and greys, swallow prominents and white satins on the remnant of the trees which had been planted there. These poplars were dying fast. I found a " nest " of baby goat moth caterpillars under a patch of loose bark.

The goat, a sturdy raw-meat coloured fellow, spends four years burrowing in a tree, eating wood, before it matures. This mother moth had blundered. There was not enough wood here for one, let alone this swarm of active little beasts. Even at that tender age I got a whiff of their peculiar billy goat-and-apple smell.

The effect on bird-life was interesting too. Those which had always been there found their homes undisturbed. A round dozen of them : — skylark, meadow pipit, yellow wagtail, yellowhammer, corn bunting *(Fig. 13)*, whinchat *(Fig. 14)*, stonechat *(Fig. 15)*, on the banks; wren and whitethroat wherever there were bush-and-bramble patches; sedge warbler and waterhen along the ditches, and a few reed warblers where the reeds grew thick enough. The last three increased as new haunts opened up for them, the others remained steady.

Trees, other than the poplars, were not affected—the pollard willows round New Zealand, the grove of ash and willow further along Reach lode. The tallest still had their carrion crow's and magpie's nests, borrowed by kestrels if any old ones were going begging. Stock

Fig. 16.
Tree Sparrows

doves, tree sparrows *(Fig. 16)*, little owls—often a barn owl—nested in the pollard holes. Except for magpies (on the increase everywhere) none of these birds was much influenced by the change.

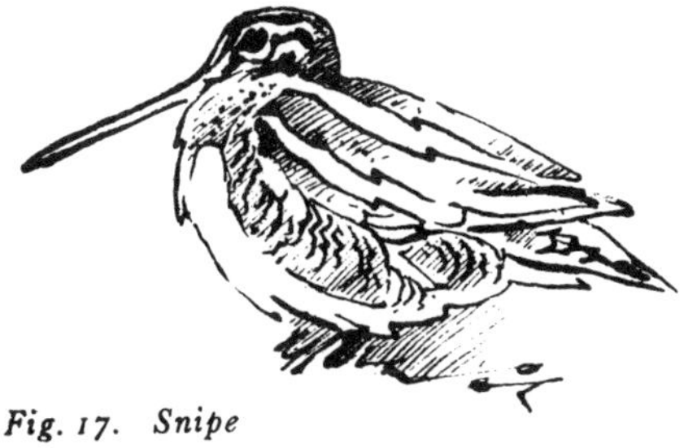

The western bit of fen which had always been neglected was less and less

Fig. 17. Snipe

disturbed by the uncertain drainage. Its choked ditches helped to hold up the water rather than waste it. Carr growth was checked. The thickets which had already taken hold got thicker and taller but no more rose beside them. There was an increase in the numbers of both wood-pigeons and turtle doves; the bushes were often visited by cuckoos and by sparrow-hawks.

None of the birds mentioned up to now (except reed warblers) had any real need to live in Adventurers Fen. A railway cutting near a wooded stream would have suited them just as well. Like the swifts and swallows for ever wheeling overhead they were not fen birds. Nor, except at certain times to suit certain species, was the fen ready for fen birds.

A few pages back I called it a testing ground. It was, for plants and insects, fishes and birds, and that is why it was so enthralling. There is a constant flux in nature, a flow towards the finding and making use of new conditions and an ebb, often reluctant and with burnt fingers, when the luck refuses to hold. Birds, free to travel and search wide tracks of country from the air, show this best. But the same urge finds a stickle-back as the water recedes stranded a yard from its ditch. Whenever the fen, see-sawing between drought and flood, had something to offer which filled their need of the moment, the birds found it. And this was not confined to those already in the neighbourhood, nor to definite migration times when the sight of water might well tempt passage terns or waders

Fig. 18. Redshank

to drop down. The guests were naturally more numerous then.

There were plenty of birds but the species varied almost from day to day. Only a few common fen birds had learned to put up with its vagaries all the year round: mallard, heron, snipe *(Fig. 17)*, waterhen, water rail

23

and, in the fragrant summer litter, sedge and grasshopper warblers.

Although at times large flocks of peewits assembled neither they nor redshanks had yet re-established themselves as breeding birds. *(Fig. 18.)* They called in with other waders, and terns, during the few weeks of spring migration. In autumn it was too dry for them: fieldfares, mistle thrushes, flocks of greenfinches, chaffinches and tree sparrows were seen instead. At harvest time turtledoves came in their hundreds to feast on the seeds and cool their pink toes in the mud at the sides of the drain. Like wood-pigeons they were thirsty birds.

In winter and early spring the flooding brought duck: mostly widgeon, now and then a fair sprinkling of mallard, shoveller, pochard and teal. Common and blackheaded gulls came in night and morning for a drink and a bathe on their way between the inland ploughs and the Wash. This forty mile trip was undertaken every day.

None of these birds showed much desire to stay. Adventurers Fen for all its loneliness was merely a place where they could feed and rest awhile. They seemed to know that presently all the water must disappear.

Only the coots and dabchicks, both very early nesters, tried to breed. It must have been very trying for a sitting coot to watch the water round her nest sink lower every day. I found dabchicks trying to dive in ditches scarcely deep enough for them to paddle in.

But it was soon to change. The pump in the ten foot drain was wearing out; the odds were heavily against replacement or even repair.

CHAPTER IV

(1930–1936)–1940: NATURE TAKES OVER

MAN gave up the unequal struggle and retired to his few acres in the north-east corner. The mill stood sentinel on the fenward boundary. It was a symbol rather than a servant since the ditches now led straight into the wide drain at the opposite end. A gale in the spring of 1937 threw it down.

The fen had not yet reached full sufficiency; it was still dependent on flood water, the amount of which varied from year to year. It was not until the winter of 1936–7, when a great flood rolled from bank to bank, that enough water remained to withstand future droughts. From then on, summer and winter, the level never varied by more than a foot. The Bailiff of Bedford had come to help Adventurers Fen re-establish itself—but that is a tale for the next chapter.

From 1930 to 1936 the fen did not dry off completely, as it had done during the previous decade. The peat was saturated and plenty of water remained at least throughout the breeding season to attract a much larger stock of birds. But the loss from seepage and evaporation was far greater than would have happened in undrained fen with its inexhaustible reserves. The reeds, now beginning to spread fast, also sucked up a great deal of moisture during their summer growth.

Nevertheless the water dwindled so slowly that some part of the fen from July onwards was always right for migrant wading birds. There was now a fair certainty of finding a given species at its appropriate time whereas before it had been a gamble.

A minor flood had tempted a spoonbill to the fen next door in 1917. In 1920 a blacknecked grebe was seen swimming along Burwell lode. Bittern, bearded tit, spotted crake and other fen birds had been recorded fairly recently from the neighbourhood, but these isolated instances meant little. Stray birds have turned up in all manner of places and will do so again. It is their permanence or seasonal recurrence in a particular place that counts.

25

A brief survey of Adventurers Fen as it lay before the flood of 1936–37 might be helpful here. *(See Map Two, inside back cover.)*

A waterlogged jungle of litter, reeds a n d s e d g e reached nearly half-way down the triangle from the western point. Except at that end the bushes were dying out and the reeds slowly strangling all lower growth. The wider basal half of the

Fig. 19. Peewit and Chicks

triangle as far as Mill Road had become one enormous reedbed. The original fields were still parcelled out by their drains and ditches since these were too deep for reeds to grow in. A fringe of open water lay beside Reach lode bank broadening out to the east of New Zealand. The cottages, empty since 1927, were falling down. Big cracks had opened in the walls and the wooden floors were smashed by horses wandering through the downstair rooms. The older cottage had withstood neglect better than the one put up fifteen years before; a monument to jerry-building.

East of Mill Road the area between it and Commissioner's Drain stood open as far north as the new pump drain, where the water was deepest. Clumps of giant sedge and various rushes broke the surface. The shallow southern side, tufted with common rush, was bordered with reeds. Between the pump drain and the cultivated land lay a series of reed-encircled pools, the water getting shallower as it neared the most recently lost fields in front of the mill.

Fig. 20. Short-eared Owl

The roads, still passable with care in gum-boots, were under water f o r three parts of the year—far easier to get about by punt

26

along the intersecting ditches. It was
a Sunday pleasaunce for the local
villagers no longer: they had to walk
round by the lode sides and along Commissioner's Drain.

Fig. 21.
Pied Wagtail

The waterweeds spread from the
ditches as fast as the reeds. In a few
seasons sheets of water were covered
yellow and white with crowfoot, pink with persicaria, gold with
bladderwort bloom; and below them the dark masses of Canadian
waterweed crept forward irresistibly. Marestail advanced more slowly;
hornwort and milfoil were reluctant to leave their ditches at all. Star-
wort rose from old turf pits where it must have lain sleeping for years.
The pits were plotted under water by its bright green clusters long after
all contour at the bottom had been smothered by the vile Canadian
weed.

The marestails and persicarias grew as cheerfully in mud when the
water shrank. They had figwort, kingcups, arrowheads and the tall
water plantains for company and such of the litter plants as survived
long immersion. Comfrey, willowherb, St. John's wort, mint and the
loosestrifes seemed best able to withstand this; especially the purple
loosestrife whose ragged spires gave a distinctive accent to large tracts of
fen.

By August most of the water from the open part of the fen had drained
away. It left acres of cracked mud under a thick felt of moss and wilting
waterweed. It was a fascinating place to roam about in. The moss
deadened the footfall: there were no dry
sticks to snap, no stalks to crackle and plenty
of good hiding-places among the islands of
reed and sallow bushes.

Fig. 22.
Yellowshank

The ditches held a little muddy water
and it was always moist under the reeds.
A tang, softer than that of a salt marsh,
escaped from the damp peat under the surface crust. The dross below the scattered
loosestrife spires was not too high to conceal
birds moving about in it.

27

There was no lack of birds. Successive broods reared on the fen broke up: young snipe, waterhens, water rails, yellow wagtails, meadow pipits were all learning to fend for themselves. The reeds and sallows were full of warblers, many of them little more than fledglings with tom-thumb tails.

Peewits brought their broods down from the uplands *(Fig. 19)*, redshanks theirs from the rushy meadows. They flew above them calling distractedly at every alarm; carrion crows, short-eared owls and harriers were ever on the prowl. *(Fig. 20.)* Rooks often passed over but they never haunted the fen like the crows. It was easy to recognize a crow: the glib flight, more fickle than the patient flapping of the rooks, and the harsh rolled caw branded him the old villain that he is. Short-eared owls hunted by day and night. Their wings were longer and less bowed than other owls'. The hesitant flight and the way they quartered the reeds made people mistake them for harriers: but they travelled so slowly and one glimpse of the head should have settled the question at once.

As summer dawdled into autumn the numbers and variety rose steadily; turtle doves, wood-pigeons, herons, pied wagtails *(Fig. 21)*, ducks, waders and gulls. The waders were the most interesting group: ducks in eclipse plumage are dull and the fen was never without its chorus of gulls.

From August onwards snipe, jacksnipe, peewits, redshanks were always present and generally with them a few golden plover, green sandpipers and ruffs (or reeves). Less frequently dunlin, ring plover, little stint, common and wood sandpipers, one of the godwits (most often the black tailed), an odd curlew or whimbrel and once, in 1934, a yellowshank from North America arrived.

It stepped from behind a tussock thirty feet away and stood balancing on thin bent yellow legs, jerking its head and watching me. *(Fig. 22.)* I think I was the more surprised.

It was a little smaller than a redshank, very slender and the whole bill —not only the tip—the least bit upturned. The plumage, of the same quiet mixture of grey and brown, had a sharper pattern—a distinctly speckled bird. The wings, as it fled away, had no broad white hind border though the white back V was very distinct. The double whistling note was subdued compared to a redshank's, more plaintive and less musical.

This yellowshank stayed either on Adventurers Fen or on a sewage farm seven miles away from March 1934 until the following February and then yellowshanks turned up in various other places until October 1936: no doubt the same bird. An encouraging sign if it means that rare birds are more likely to be watched than shot as they were forty years ago.

In most years one or two pairs of Montagu harriers breed on Wicken Fen. *(Fig. 23.)* There was so much thick cover at Wicken that they came to hunt in Adventurers instead.

A hunting harrier flew low—less than ten feet above the sedges. A few calm beats interrupted the periods of sailing along with wings raised forward, partly flexed, the primary tips spaced like the open fingers of a hand. The long tail normally remained closed. The width of wing-spread and continual veering of the bird gave the impression of slow, wavering flight, but nevertheless a long stretch of fen was traversed steadily in a short time. The legs were carried loosely; instead of being tucked away to trim the hull, one or both would often be let down as if to limber them in instant readiness for action.

A turtle dove is no fool at flying; it springs neatly off the mark and can twist with lightning speed.

It puzzled me to find little piles of their feathers about the place and always with the stumpy footprint of a Montagu tell-tale in the mud beside them. So I watched to find out why. Along came the Montagu *(Fig. 24)*, almost brushing the reed tops, making for one of the taller oases of reed: spurted over the top and into the fairway in a twinkling, darting left or right to snatch a dove before it had time to get clear.

Montagu harriers were summer migrants. They had gone by mid-October but the gap was already filled by two or three hen harriers taking up winter quarters on the fen. They sometimes hunted in couples, flying some twenty yards apart, each ready to pounce on anything disturbed by the other. *(Fig. 25.)* It was amazing how swiftly they struck. They turned on a threepenny bit and flicked themselves down in a flash. A small bird in the danger zone had to be quick but was safe if it got away before the claw shot down. These harriers chased nothing that flew faster than themselves. They would follow and make dive after dive at a vole dodging in the grass but if a small bird eluded the first rush it was given up. The harrier swore and returned to the tactics that served it best.

Fig. 23. *Montagu Harrier*

They were more bluff in build than the lightweight Montagus and more compact than the marsh harriers. *(Fig. 26, and see Fig. 55.)* An old cock in its gull-grey uniform with jet-black wingtips and white rump was a glorious bird. More than once, waiting in the reeds, I had one sail past near enough to catch the alert expression in its yellow eye.

The brown " ringtails "—females and immatures—had the broad white band at the root of the tail but many Montagus had some white there as well: the heavier build and steadier flight were better distinguishing points.

Adventurers Fen soon filled again with the November rains. The water gleamed more brightly every day as the level rose and the night frosts stripped the flag off the reeds. The winter duck came in—mallard, shoveler, wigeon, teal and, in the deeper water, small companies of pochard and tufted duck. Apart from occasional pintail no other kind came in winter until the flood in 1936. If they did they were not seen in the silver and brown expanse of water and reeds.

There were thousands of coots, hundreds of dabchicks and up to a dozen mute swans—perhaps two adult pairs, the rest grey-washed immatures. A good many of these birds stayed on in the spring to breed: not all of them, an area twenty times the size of Adventurers Fen would have been needed.

Perhaps 50 pairs of mallard, 30 of shoveler (400 shoveler were once seen and, at times, there

Fig. 24. *Montagu Harrier and Turtle Doves*

30

Fig. 25. Pair of Hen Harriers

may have been even larger flocks of mallard and wigeon present in early spring) and 10 pairs each of pochard and garganey would be all the fen could maintain.   Wigeon and pintail do not normally breed in southern England and the fen was not ideal for tufted duck and teal.   A few nested however, and in 1938 a pair of gadwall reared a brood.

A hundred pairs of duck in all, half as many water rails and dabchicks, twice as many coots and waterhens is a fair estimate.   Add to that at least a hundred pairs each of sedge and reed warblers, and a colony of, say, one hundred and fifty pairs of blackheaded gulls.   What with the rest of the small fry and odd kestrels, waders, crows, doves, swans, pheasants and partridges the fen had a good deal to provide.

Far exceeding these were the starlings who gathered to roost in the reeds.   They got their living from miles around but the fen gave them sanctuary at night.   Some were picked off by little owls; castings, each capped with the beak and crushed head and made of the starling's feathers, littered the upper floors of the old cottages at New Zealand.

A pair of merlins *(Fig. 27)* always spent the winter on the fen.   They, too, took toll of the starling hordes until December when the bare trampled reedbeds were deserted for warmer thicket-roosts elsewhere.

Sometimes, when the starlings left in the mornings, a sparrowhawk darted from the cover of the willow trees and took one from the fringe of a flock. There was a sudden uprush in the air, a glimpse of barred spreadeagled wings and tail and the hawk turned away with a starling squawking in its claws. *(Fig. 28.)*

I never saw a kestrel take a starling. One year they nested in the gutterhead of a broken drainpipe on one of the cottages. It had cradled a pair of young stockdoves the year before. The gutterhead hung at a precarious angle and wobbled as the young kestrels moved about. But it held even though the youngest—we called him Benjamin—was left in the nest for a week after his brothers and sisters had gone.

Most hawks and owls begin to incubate as soon as the first egg is laid and the chicks hatch out at intervals. The demands of growing appetites are thus conveniently spread.

Benjamin on his first flight looked more like an owl than a hawk. *(Fig. 29.)* His head was muffled in a bonnet of grey down, his tail and quills but three-parts grown. The wings were rounded at the ends, not pointed. To forestall accidents next year the gutter was pulled down. The kestrels nested on the rafters near a hole in the roof instead.

New Zealand, leaky, dirty, draughty as a sieve was nevertheless the rallying point. We hid our lunches there, spare cartridges and scythes, upstairs out of the horses' way, and moored the punt to its girdle of willows. A belt of black mud, once a garden, stood between them and the cottages to keep small boys away: we had gum-boots.

At dawn on summer Sundays, Ernest, the keeper and I would push the punt up narrow ditches under reeds sagging drenched with dew. Everything had to be stowed aboard: baccy, breakfast, gun to greet a roving carrion crow, scythes, rub and beer—there wasn't a dry spot anywhere else to lay your chattles on. Sedge warblers chittered from the borders of the ditches *(Fig. 30)*, but out in the reedbeds all was very still. The cries of gulls and coots, the whinnying of dabchicks came from another world. Ours only held the rippling crackle of the scythes, the swish of falling swathes, the rasp of sharpening and a curse when the scythe-point stuck in an underwater stub. Yellow wagtails came dancing over the reeds to alight and patter along the floating swathes. *(Fig. 31.)*

We were clearing wide spaces in the reedbeds for flighting duck. Hitherto it had been impossible to gather more than a few of those duck which fell into thick cover when shot. Standing in tall reed it was difficult to judge the spot and give the dog a fair start: the dense jungle of matted reed stems in two to three feet of water beat all but stout-hearted dogs in any case. With every care in allowing for wind and choosing a shot some duck fell wide and were lost. And men who stand unruffled by driven partridges are apt to get excited when duck come twirling out of the half-light overhead.

These new pools certainly improved the pick-up when the fen was shot over—four or five times—next season. A patch of reed was left uncut round the hide in the middle of each pool for a blind and the gun had open water for thirty or forty yards all round him.

The duck enjoyed the pools between whiles. Except on shooting days they were quiet, remote and well screened from passers-by on the lode banks. Whichever way the wind blew one side broke its force and the duck could rest and preen in comfort. The drifts of little feathers and muddied water showed how much the pools were used.

I confess I enjoyed the making of them as much as the shooting, if not more.

There is an art in handling a scythe. It is no fancy tool but a man's possession, rusty and often wormeaten, packed with odd nails and bits of leather. These are no makeshift dodges to overcome slack fittings: the play is meant to be there and to be taken up as the scythe is set for the job in hand at the moment.

(*Fig. 32.*) The shank of the blade is bent and lies along the stick heel for a little way before it bends again to enter the " cray " hole. An iron ring binds shank to stick as near the end as possible. Both ring and cray hole must be wedged to tighten them: the spread and angle of the blade depend on where and how far those wedges are driven in—a strip of old boot leather one-sixteenth of an inch thick, well hammered home, can make all the difference between good and indifferent mowing.

Each of the wooden handles, or tholes, is pierced by an iron shaft with a ring by which it can be slid down the stick and wedged into position. The shaft of the upper handle runs straight from the ring; that of the lower is bent at right angles and this transmits a pull to keep the point of the blade up as it sweeps round. The upper one (for the left hand) is set out nearly parallel with the blade; the other one comes farther round to the front. Their position on the stick depends partly on the

stature of the mower and partly
on what he intends to mow. If
the lower is too low your arm
begins to ache in half an hour;
if the upper is too high you get a
backache.

For mowing at ground level
they are set by ready measure.
With the scythe heel in the right
armpit swing the arm across the
stick; the outstretched fingers
should just not touch the lower
handle. Now lay the back of the

Fig. 26. Male Hen Harrier

forearm with half-clenched hand between the
handles; the distance should be that between the
elbow and the second row of knuckles.

For reed-cutting we set the blade " pulled in
and looking up at you," and lowered the handles.
The reeds were growing in two feet of water and
so couldn't be cut at ground level. Before beginning to mow, the stay (which hooks in a hole on
the blade and goes to a ring on the stick) had to
be taut and the edge razor-fine.

The scythe was set up on end and the blade
steadied under the left arm. The right hand

Fig. 27. Merlin

*Fig. 28. Sparrowhawk
taking Starling*

34

Fig. 29.
" Benjamin "—
A Young Kestrel

held the rub—twenty strokes inside and out given alternately as far as the rub would reach, laying it to the rib, not the edge. By striking the rib, the curve of the rub put just the right finish on the edge below. A little extra polish on the point and the edge tanged sweetly all along when tested with a finger-tip.

We tried the wind and cut a long lane through the reedbed. This was the hardest job. The falling reeds had no-where to fall, they bunched and hindered the follow through. After that it was easier. The wind, coming over our right

Fig. 30. Sedge Warbler

shoulders, pressed each " clip " of reeds against the sweep of the blade and blew it clear when cut. There was no need for a " bale." This was a tough willow wand bent in a half-hoop and lashed to the stick above

Fig. 31. Yellow Wagtail.

the blade. It was put there to gather and push the " clip " aside when cutting litter or hay.

If the point stuck in an unseen sallow stub it had to be coaxed out gingerly. A bent blade can be straightened out but will never stand up to hard work again.

We kept our scythes sharp. As soon as the edge showed as a thin white line it was time to " touch her up." (*Fig. 33.*) The white line meant that the edge had got blurred by the thick, hard stems.

35

Mowing looks so easy and effortless. Effortless it is—arms and scythe move as one; a surge from the shoulders, a swing from the hips and the keen blade needs no more. Left foot forward, step by step: the tall reeds totter and fall. But it is not easy—at first. Nor are reeds the best stuff to begin on. They are heavy and tough and there is a tendency to take too generous a clip. This makes the scythe hang instead of snicking sweetly through. Sedge is the beginner's joy; it should slice like butter with a well-found scythe.

We made stands out of the timber of New Zealand's barn. The thatch and laths had rotted away. We pulled the rafters and woodwork down, sawed them into convenient lengths and stowed them on the punt. One stand-full at a time: four posts for the corners; four bearers to nail between them and build a platform on; an extra post on one side for the " door "; lengths of planking from the gable ends to make the floor; and three double rows of lath across each side to hold the walls of reed which made the hide complete. To drive in the posts an old table was taken for standing on, with planks nailed to its feet to stop it sinking in the mud. Hammers, saws and nails—plenty of nails, every one dropped in the water was gone for good—that was the load collected and piled on the punt. The outward journeys took longer than coming back.

It was good fun and the hides still stood in 1941, derelict in a dry, fire-blackened land. I'm afraid I got more pleasure from those hides than the others who merely shot from them—despite the fact that duckflight-ing at dawn counts highest of all with most men who go shooting. That was because we built them, Ernest the keeper and I, in the peace of Sunday mornings. We cut the pools, we made plank bridges over ditches that ran six feet deep below the level of the peat, itself two feet below surface level. We knew every inch of the fen.

It was good to be there in the dank of the reeds, in the hush of earliest morning. We loosed the punt and slid her from her moorings, out across the open water as the duck began to flight home from their feeding places. They used Adventurers Fen to rest in in the daytime. At night they left, hundreds of them setting out at dusk to feed on the washes and stubbles. Some stayed close by on the surrounding fenland; others, travelling high in skeins and uneven Vs and Ws spread half-way across the sky, went farther afield.

It was too dark when we started to see the first flights coming home: we heard them muttering overhead, their faint wing-whisper and the tearing as they slithered down, the muffled splashes as they took the water. And presently, as the light grew stronger, we could see them— blurred shapes racing past us in the dwindling starlight; black and clean-cut as they wheeled to string across the first pale wedge of morning in the east.

We took our guns—our twenty-bores and a few cartridges—although, unless for a chance carrion crow, we seldom used them. Except in windy weather when the rustling of the reeds and the wind itself destroys the noise, indiscriminate shooting should never be allowed on a duck marsh. Ducks are easily upset. On still days the echo of a shot carries far across the surface and the patter of spent pellets on the water soon disturbs them.

We poled the punt to where we meant to work, through channels where stray reeds and sallow branches scraped quietly down its sides, along ditches overhung between thick reedbeds. The cold stems brushed our arms and faces, drenching us with dew.

We set to work building hides, or took our scythes from where they had been lying in the reeds. Leaving a scythe in water for a time does no harm to the blade. It keeps the stick swollen and the fastenings firm —a few touches with a rub will fetch the rust off and bring the edge up keen as ever again. They should never be left where children might run against them, or a casual passer-by be tempted to pick one up and try to use it.

The sun climbed out of the morning haze. Its low beams lit the fringes of the pool and warmed the air. It had risen high enough to dry the reeds before we stopped for breakfast. We sat there on the long grey nose of the duck punt, legs dangling in the water—one if not both soaked through in spite of thighlong waterboots—content as only men knew how to be who are happiest in their oldest clothes, munching bread and cheese and drinking beer.

There were admittedly some minor troubles of the fen—biting midges and mosquitoes; horseflies with their chequered wings and transparent green-gold eyes; dull grey clegs who settled unbeknown and got their blow in first; capsized punts and sprawlings in the mud; slinkings-home in sodden, reeking clothes and squelching gumboots. Such trivialities only came to redouble the joy of all the rest.

Fig. 33.
" Touching her up "

Fig. 32. A well-found Scythe

We did not always use the hides when shooting. The duck became aware of them towards the end of the season. They circled high above the fen when they came in on a winter morning and pitched well out of gunshot of the pools.

It was better not to shoot the place at all during the daytime but to wait for the flight out in the evening. Still nights were useless. The duck went over three or four gunshots high but, if we had judged their line of flight correctly, there was plenty of shooting in rough windy weather—plenty of shooting, but not necessarily much to show for all the expenditure of powder.

38

CHAPTER V

1930–(1936–1940): THE BAILIFF OF BEDFORD WINS

Fig. 34. Blackheaded Gull Chick

MEN of the fens are used to floods. One way and another they've had to deal with them all their lives and seldom but what a crop of some sort came from the flooded land in the end.

The flood of 1936–37 was a bad one: you stood and saw nothing but water around for miles and miles, but it was worse, far worse, in the daily papers than in the fen. Day and night for weeks they patrolled the banks, levelling a low place here with rows of sandbags, stopping a weak place there with a buttress of wattle and clay. If a serious crack threatened it was sealed by towing a barge-load of ballast across it and sinking the barge. For a day or two high tides at Denver Sluice prevented

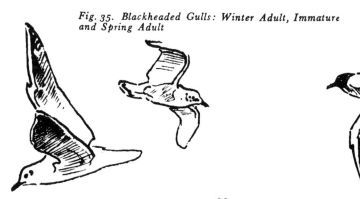

Fig. 35. Blackheaded Gulls: Winter Adult, Immature and Spring Adult

39

the water from getting away for more than a few hours out of the twenty-four. It was touch and go.

But in all those thousands of miles of banked-up waterways there were only two small breaks and, as the fenmen said, they made a rare fuss over that.

Adventurers Fen was not threatened; it was full from bank to bank in any case. The water strayed south for a field or two across the low track from High Town bridge to the Reach lode bank. The tops of the fence posts marked the track—excellent perches for gulls.

Many gulls began building their nests on the tufts of rush rising above the water in these fields. Blackheaded gulls liked having water all round them but felt safer with some anchorage for the nest. A fortnight later they were all left high and dry. This had happened before on the fen itself since the birth of a colony there in 1933—six nests built on open patches of water between high reeds. By 1937 nearly three hundred gulls were breeding, scattered about the fen in groups of ten to fifty pairs.

Blackheaded gulls nest on islands and coastal marrams but for choice they are marsh-nesting birds. They were quick to take advantage of any favouring circumstance. When cutting pools in the reedbeds we left long lines of floating swathes: by next morning the gulls had been pulling loose ends together and within a week there were eggs in nests all down the lines. To keep the colony within reasonable limits the first two clutches were taken; the third was allowed to hatch. The chicks in black and brown marbled down scrambled from their nests to hide in the rushes within an hour of being born. *(Fig. 34.)* Many eggs and chicks were stolen by magpies and carrion crows. Rats (brown rats leading a watery life, not vegetarian water voles) and pike took others so not many were reared. These rats were as versatile in their habits as the gulls. They made nests—closely woven bundles of dry grass as big as footballs—in the middle of thick sedge clumps, above water level but hundreds of yards from the nearest dry land. I have thrust my hand into these balls expecting to count duck's eggs: ducks build in similar places and always cover their eggs cosily before leaving them. A squirming litter of naked baby rats was felt instead.

Later on the lucky chicks flapped round the pools on short, uncertain wings. Even when fully fledged they were easy to tell from their parents: wings, shoulders and tails were marked with soft brown bars and the head had a few dark spots instead of the adult brown mask. In autumn the adults lost their masks and retained one dark patch behind and below the eye. Their plumage otherwise was unaltered.

The wings of a blackheaded gull look sharper than other gulls' wings of similar size. They are, and the effect is heightened by their colour scheme. A narrow flash of silvery-white along the leading edge is backed by a strip of black shading into the grey. There is no black triangle tipped with white at the wingtip, as in a kittiwake or common gull, to hinder the streamline effect. The blackheaded's bill and feet are dusky crimson, both the others' some shade of yellow-green. *(Fig. 35.)*

Holidays were taken in spring. That was the best time for birds and we went to all manner of out-of-the-way places in search of them.

In 1937 Adventurers Fen held so many interesting kinds that my tent was pitched on Reach lode bank with plenty of note-book and sketching material to hand. Gear was always reduced to a minimum: tent, groundsheet, field glasses, paints and paper and the bare essentials of food and clothing. There was a plentiful supply of coots' and gulls' eggs and no lack of water for the kettle.

At dawn everything that would be wanted for the day was put aboard the punt before pushing out among the reeds. Before leaving the tent it was as well to raise the skirt cautiously and look all round. This often brought a subject for a sketch; field mice doing acrobatics on the guys or young herons preening thirty yards away. *(Fig. 36.)*

The tent, deserted all day, lost its human association and was accepted as part of the landscape. It was seldom visited again before evening.

Night and day the fen re-echoed with the calls of the water-birds. One night the rumble of thunder crept up from the east and, as the storm rolled nearer, the cries of the birds increased. Before it reached the zenith the whole fen was a babel of noise: gull, coot, shoveler, garganey, but the neigh upon neigh of the dabchicks was the sound that led them all. Then came absolute silence awaiting the rip—crash—crackle of a clap right overhead. I turned up the edge of my groundsheet as the first thud of rain struck the tent.

For the second half of the holiday my wife joined me. We decided to explore a wider area of flooded fen and the middle reaches of the Ouse where the Bailiff of Bedford dwelt. There wasn't much room in the gun-punt when all had been packed aboard.

Fig. 36. Young Herons Preening

At the start we ran into a thunderstorm as we pulled through Upware Lock into the Cam. A string of barges passed heading our way. We hitched to the hindmost and towed to the Dog and Duck where the Old West river ran in. Camp was made that night in the lee of a hawthorn hedge beside the bank a little way up the Old West. Dead thorn branches broken from among living boughs crackled cheerfully under the pot though the night was wet.

By Elford Closes and Twenty Pence Bridge, past miles of drowned washes and grey-beared rushes, miles of winding banks where the spate had scoured the earth and freshened the grass, we came to Earith and the Ouse. The lock-keeper was amused. We bounced like a cork on the swirl as the great lock filled – five – ten – fifteen – nearly twenty feet, for the water stood high in the

Fig. 37. "Slid out into the broad shining Ouse"

42

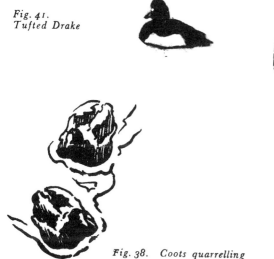

Fig. 41.
Tufted Drake

Fig. 39. Coots:
Adult, Immature and Chick

Fig. 38.   Coots quarrelling

Fig. 40. Great Crested Grebe

river above.   The gates swung slowly open and the little punt slid into the broad, shining Ouse. *(Fig. 37.)*

Away to the east the Hundred Foot lay like a streak of silver in its thirty mile channel to Lynn.   But we turned west, keeping out of the strong main stream in slacker water near the bank.   That night we camped by an osier bed and reed warblers sang all round us until dawn. Past flooded gardens and fields of buttercups stem-deep in water, past Bluntisham Lock, wide open to the flood, to Overcote.   We cut corners over the fields, floating through hedges and trees; it was easier to punt across the shallows than to row against midstream.   We bathed and watched the young entry from a heronry fishing and perching clumsily on half-submerged trees.

St. Ives Lock stood on an island.   We sidetracked it by a quarter-mile over flooded meadows and tied up downstream of the bridge.   The water was almost washing the crown of the centre arch, there wasn't a hope of getting through.   What could the boatyard people suggest?   They hadn't allowed a punt out there for the last ten days: a boat and four men had gone over Hemingford Weir, but the water should waste in a few more days.   A few more days!—that was no use to us.

43

We persuaded a lorry to carry the punt to Houghton Mill, avoiding the weirs, and got her afloat again. The narrow tongue of bank between the bypass and the lock was the driest place for camp. We spent two nights there listening to the triple roar of water through bypass, mill-stream and lock. Another night was spent by Brampton Mill, and on next day to Offord where we had to get the rollers out, pushing the punt up a slipway and over the road.

The flood was lessening along the wooded reaches to St. Neots: the Ouse became its lazy self again. Many birds were seen during the journey but neither in numbers nor variety to equal the wealth on Adventurers Fen.

Here in the early spring of 1937 the surface was dotted with fowl and the lode banks sprinkled white with resting gulls: the majority black-headed, but one in four a common, and perhaps one in forty a herring gull. These large gulls seldom came so far inland.

Their arch-enemy, a big brown skua, had followed and was plying his trade. Singling out a gull the skua chased it, hanging relentlessly a yard off its tail, stooping, bullying, until the gull threw up its meal to get away. The skua, twisting with surprising swiftness for a heavy bird, dived and caught the food in the air. And then planed down to the water to enjoy a half-digested eel.

In places the surface was black with coots. Some of them were already cruising round with wings arched above stern and lowered head. These were males guarding a territory around the future nest-site. They rushed at trespassers with mighty splashings and explosive sounds but the attack was not driven home. Both birds sheered off and as they swam apart the ruffled feathers quietened down. *(Fig. 38.)*

The coots built nests, substantial piles of broken reeds and rushes, at intervals all down the rows of reeds marking the old field ditches. These were the favourite sites. The old bird sitting on her nest could see all round her and be seen. Coots don't bother to conceal their eggs like waterhens. Incidentally coots' eggs are very good to eat.

Every island of sedge or rushes of any size, every belt of reeds in the open water held a coot's nest and they built all round our flighting pools, a little way back from the edge. They insisted on open water, if only a ditch, and avoided the middle of thick reedbeds where waterhens and rails were content to nest.

The down of the baby coot's head was covered with long, yellow filaments tipped with waxy-red " nits "—a ginger halo seen against the sun. Their queer lobed feet looked many times too large. Later on the young bird wore a white bib and waistcoat; the black plumage and shining head-shield were not achieved until after the first moult. *(Fig. 39.)* Coots' eyes are ruby red but you had to get close to see them.

There were often a few pintail among the wigeon flocks. The drakes' fronts gleamed as bright spots when the pattern of all other waterfowl was lost in distance haze. The shoveler's white breast was conspicuous but did not carry so far; the coot's bald patch still less.

A lone cock wigeon or pintail occasionally stayed well on into May, long after the rest had gone. Nesting was never proved although young examples of both were seen—and some shot—early in September. But these birds were full-winged and might as easily have been the first new-comers from the north on autumn passage.

We had visits from other ducks which normally live round the coasts: four shelducks and a pair of scaup in 1938, a smew in 1939 and three goosanders fishing in Burwell lode in 1940.

By the beginning of May the fen had settled down. The return to primitive fen conditions was complete: open water, sheltered pools, low tangled marsh, high beds of reeds and, round the margin by the lodes, a damp and flowery no-man's-land. Each once more became the home of many of its original plants and birds.

The open water lay round the south-east corner. It was between four and five feet deep. The two characteristic plants were giant sedge, growing in isolated clumps, and water crowfoot which spread its sheets of white and yellow flowers between the clumps in June. The sedge stems, bearing loose-knit sprays of little scaley flowers, stood eight feet high above the dull green drooping leaves. These felt harsh to the touch and their edges cut like knives.

This was the playground of the diving birds: coot, pochard, tufted duck, great crested grebe. *(Fig. 40.)* It is hard to say why this grebe did not breed: scores of dabchicks did and even the blacknecked grebe. I think, in time, they would have founded a colony. It so happened that single birds arrived, stayed for a few weeks and left, not finding a mate.

Tufted ducks had long been winter visitors and in 1937 two pairs bred. I found a nestful of their grey-green eggs in the shrivelled debris at the base of a great clump of sedge.

Fig. 42. " Five Pochard Drakes swam behind a Duck "

In April a pair of them, the dingy duck and her squat little black and white drake, had drifted away from the flock for longer and longer each day. *(Fig. 41.)* He rode on the water alone in the first week of May never far from the clump where the duck was beginning to brood.

Six ducklings hatched, balls of sooty-brown and dusky-yellow fluff, and scuttled away to the shelter of the sedges behind their mother.

Pochards were always more numerous than tufted ducks.

Spring put a new burnish on the sleek red heads of the drakes, whitened their flanks and wheedled a hint of tenderness into the harsh " kurr." Five drakes swam behind a duck. Each pretended he hadn't noticed her and was swimming that way by chance. But the little red eyes were watchful : no sooner had one manœuvred himself into position beside her than the others were after him, bobbing their heads and jostling to cut him out. *(Fig. 42.)*

Fig. 43.   Pochard Drake in Flight

Most pochard ducks are drab and blotchy in appearance, like the drake in eclipse, but this one had a distinct cream circlet round the base of her bill.   Her plumage, though duller, was nearly as well-defined as a male's.

These diving ducks have big strong paddles, and short narrow wings set well back on the body.   They cannot spring neatly from the surface but squatter along it to take off, kicking coot-fashion with the feet as well. Their necks are short and thick, their bodies heavy and broad, but once under way this clumsiness can be coaxed into a fine burst of speed. *(Fig. 43.)*

Pochards look at their best on a frosty April morning, whizzing past in a flock so evenly spaced that another bird could scarcely be fitted in without collision.   Each bullneck stretches poker-stiff in front, the leaden feet strain either side the tail behind, the wings flash mealy-grey as they wheel in unison over the morning ice.

On still days it was pleasant to drift across this open water in the punt. Pike darted away unseen but known by the arrowy wedge creasing the surface ahead.   They probably ate each other since there were very few

Fig. 44.   Wild Duck and Brood

Fig. 45.   Teal

47

other fish. A grass snake swimming across made a different pattern: the little crooked knob of its head was followed by corkscrew ripples as the rest of it wriggled steadily forward under water.

Two pairs of swans nested on the fen every year. The master pair claimed this territory. They built their nest—a pile of reeds that we could walk about on—back in the reeds and led their cygnets among the rushes round the borders. The cob came out to tidy himself and feed: his favourite rest was a high shelf on Mill Road. It was spattered with excrement and big white feathers. He didn't like the punt but moved ahead discreetly, turning his head from side to side, complaining hoarsely.

*   *   *   *

I loved the smaller, quiet pools best. There were more than a dozen of them scattered up and down the fen. Some were linked by wide and winding channels. Some lay alone: a reedy ditch just wide enough to take the punt led to them. In many ways these pools were the essence of Adventurers Fen. No two alike, the size and shape, the depth, the plants that hemmed them round and grew in them, the life they held, all differed—not fundamentally but in the proportion or profusion of whatever they held.

Those that were walled high with old reed had clean-cut margins and were still on a windy day. Their water was either deep and clear brown or fleet and strewn with shoots of young reed, loosestrifes and sallows. These were the best places to find mallard and teal.

However cautious the approach all activity in a pool ceased for a while. Then presently a rustle here, a chirrup there told of confidence restored. A wild duck spoke softly in the reeds and was answered by the whimpering of her brood. She stayed invisible but they began to filter through the stems and were soon spread in a frenzy of flycatching all over the surface. She came out too and waited at the edge, head high and giving a reassuring chuckle now and then.

A shadow swept across. One quack of alarm and she slipped back into the reeds with the ducklings packed in a thrusting rabble at her wake. *(Fig. 44.)* Ducklings were seldom taken by the harriers.

A teal dropped in without a sound, floating alert for half a minute before dipping its bill to sip. *(Fig. 45.)* They always flew more easily than larger ducks. The trim body and long flexible wings allowed them to

48

spring up and get away as instantly as snipe. Duck in any case are more nimble in the air than their build suggests. They can scratch their heads in mid-air like gulls: one was seen to twist her head round and nibble at her back. She must have had the devil of an itch.

Sometimes a teal dashed in to pitch abruptly; another would circle round first, jauntily as a butterfly, and alight with fastidious care. The flash of the white underside was conspicuous in flight.

On the water the pattern did not carry well. They looked just dark until they happened to veer round and get caught all-square in sunlight. Then the dark chestnut head and green slash on the drake's cheek, the black and emerald speculum (worn by the duck as well) lit up for a moment. At other times the creamy shoulder stripe and black-rimmed yellow wedges below the tail were the only salient points of the little drake. Their low piping was the merriest sound of the fen.

Most of the smaller pools were more open to the sky. Their margins were ill-defined and wandered in and out between beds of different rushes.

Two of the pools were ringed with reedmace. Both kinds flourished: the tall neat stems of the lesser mace were compact and they grew closer together than the bold sheaves of the poker. Their beds were dense but airy since the leaves, pliant as whipcords, let in the light to play among the stems. Their heads too were dainty, less than half the girth of the fat brown-velvet pokers.

These pokers stood as individuals, each new sheaf rising from a palisade of last year's whitened stems and leaves. Many heads rode out the winter gales and shed their fluff across the firm green cylinders of the next year's growth.

Townspeople call the pokers or reedmace " bulrushes," but this is incorrect. The true bulrush (Scirpus) is that tall, dark-green, pipe-stem reed which droops in a bold curve and bears a sparse cluster of seeds at the tip of the stem. They were uncommon on the fen itself but many fine beds grew along Reach lode, towards Upware.

Other pools, still less enclosed, were surrounded by sedges and bur-reed. The sorting-out of the different sedges was a botanist's nightmare: on the Sedge Fen at Wicken, apart from the all-pervading Cladium, nearly twenty kinds of other sedges (Carex) had been found, and most of these appeared on Adventurers Fen. Bur-reed was easily known; the

49

Fig. 48. Black Terns, Swifts and Water Bat

Fig. 46. Pair of Shoveler

Fig. 47. Garganey Drakes asleep

BLACKNECKED GREBES
BURWELL 1938
(ADVENTURERS FEN)

SLAVONIAN GREBE
STOKKESEYRI, ICELAND 1936

(NOTE ESPECIALLY DIFFERENCE IN SHAPE OF BILL)

Fig. 49. Blacknecked (and Slavonian) Grebe

flat, coarse-ribbed leaves sheathed the zig-zag stems and curled round the stalked clusters of burrs. It made dense cover, a sure place for a waterhen's nest when we wanted a few eggs for tea.

The more open the pools the more cluttered with waterweed; bladderwort, marestail and the floating lance-leaved trails of persicaria.

These were the garganey and shoveler pools: the most evident ducks of the fen. Not the most numerous but the most often seen, since both were restless birds and often on the wing.

The shoveler drake especially was a showy bird. *(Fig. 46.)* It had a big dark wedge-shaped head, white front, pale blue patches on the wings and a broad band of dusky chestnut underneath shading to auburn as it curved up round the flanks. His call was a short bass " quark " as befitted his heavy bill.

The garganey, a summer migrant, was smaller than a shoveler; but a little larger and heavier-winged than a teal. The drake had a brilliant white stripe either side of the crown. As it sat on the water the contrast between the cherry-brown foreparts and pale flanks was sharply defined. In flight, even a long way away, it had a pale, shimmery look due to the white-edged speculum and the frosty-grey wash over most of the rest of the wing.

I got within ten yards of a little drake asleep in a pool one morning. The rising sun was level with the reed tops. By keeping it dead in line behind I approached unseen quietly through breast-high cover.

He lay at anchor swaying as a light wind touched him first on one quarter, then the other. His bill was buried between the scapular feathers which curled down to meet the swell of his flanks, completely hiding the wings. The long scapulars were lavender and each feather had a white shaft-streak edged with black. *(Fig. 47.)*

I did several sketches before he woke and fled creaking from the pool. This creaking note of the garganey was a curious sound: it reminded me of tightening the wooden screw of an old linen press. It was more dry and deliberate than the rattle of nightjars or a grasshopper warbler's reel.

In the second half of May we looked for black terns. Up to about a hundred years ago they bred in fenland—the 1830-40s—when so many fen birds vanished, thanks to the activities of the Adventurers. But every year during migration time a few called in and stayed for a day or two about the pools.

Migrating birds may collect in large numbers at a halting place and then, after waiting for favourable weather, move on together in big flocks. But by far the greater part of migration must take place as a gradual movement over a wide front: parties of birds travelling in the same general direction over a period of weeks or even months.

And so, as terns passed over East Anglia, some from each wave stopped to feed and recoup themselves wherever they saw a good place. Common and arctic as well as black terns found Adventurers Fen, but we loved the black terns best. *(Fig. 48.)*

Attractive in themselves with sloe-black foreparts, white undersides and pale smoke-grey wings and tails, their flight was still more beautiful to watch.

One evening at the end of May 1939 I took the punt into one of the larger pools, wedged it among the reedmace and sat down. Fourteen black terns, a mob of swifts and three or four of the big water bats who lived in the pollard willows were wheeling overhead. *(Fig. 48.)* They were all too intent on the evening meal—moths and stoneflies hatching and rising from the rushes and sedges—to worry about me. The swifts raced everywhere at the same level, a foot above the sedge: their urgent winnow cast a rippling net across the fen in which the dull bats seemed to flutter and get caught. The terns flew higher, floating with infrequent beats until an insect soaring from a sedge tip whipped them into action. Then with a sudden lunge which sent them yards they swooped, sprang up, even turned somersaults to catch it.

The black tern does not usually hover and dive for fry as the shore terns do. It is a marsh bird. Insects are its mainstay, taken by hawking to and fro over the reed plumes or snatched from the surface as it sweeps across the water.

A stretch of water, half-fringed with reed and flanked by willows, lay near the bank by New Zealand: it was the nursery of a pair of black-necked grebes. These birds, which do not nest in eastern England and are rare elsewhere, paid a compliment to the quality of Adventurers Fen. Three of them had spent the winter diving with the tufted ducks and coots. One left, the others held their courtship on the open water and chose this corner of the fen to rear a family later on.

One Sunday morning I had let the punt drift and strand itself on a stubble of sedge close to their courting place. I lay all day under the

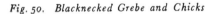

Fig. 50. Blacknecked Grebe and Chicks

Fig. 51. Dabchick: Adult and Young

canvas cover sketching them through a lowered section of coaming less than twenty yards away. *(Fig. 49.)*

They were larger but more delicate than dabchicks. The steep forehead and tip-tilted bill gave them a comical expression—the blend of imp and cherubim met in a small freckled boy. The bill, flattened from above downwards, was slender in profile. (A slavonian grebe's, compressed the other way, looks arched, like a razorbill's.)

Their neat black horns and cheek ruffs were parted by two yellow fans running back from the eyes. Their eyes were a brilliant ruby red. The black neck and breast were defined sharply from the white underside; less cleanly in the female than in the male. The golden chestnut of her flanks was not so bright as his and she was dingier on the back.

Grebes and coots build rafts to rest on in the rushes and they were making one. The male would swim away, dive beside a rush clump and come back with an offering of torn shreds dangling from his bill. Sometimes she went to meet him and whenever they came near the raft together, both would spread their shining ruffs and horns and their glistening yellow fans, bow and touch bill to bill. The ceremony often lead to antics of wild excitement. They would chase each other, leap on the raft and tread.

The female firmed the raft by squirming on her tummy and, jumping out of the water, flopped on it with a smack. They used it to rest and preen on and to exercise their wings, rearing up and flapping rapidly for

Fig. 53. Heron

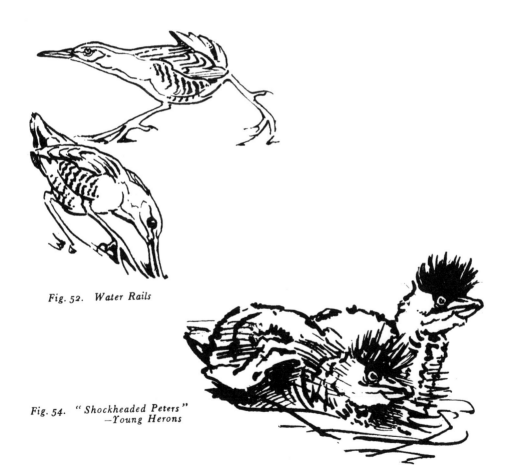

Fig. 52. Water Rails

Fig. 54. "Shockheaded Peters"
—Young Herons

twenty seconds at a time. Broad white wing-bars hitherto unseen were then disclosed.

We hoped it might have been the basis of a nest but they left the open water and, later on, the male was seen alone, setting out on fishing trips from the reeds beside New Zealand. For fear of disturbance we did not search for a nest.

Three weeks afterwards they were found early one morning in a pool close by. It was full of coots and dabchicks feeding young of various ages. The hen grebe rode high with her feathers fluffed out, never attempting to dive. The cock was diving frequently and bringing her his catch. There were no babies. The pool was cluttered with reeds and steamy with mist but presently she drifted to a clearing and he followed her with food. As he drew alongside a head shot out from her back: a tiny snakey grebeling took the food and jacked back in its box. The day was as yet too cold for babies to leave the pram.

They drew into the reeds but I stayed on, seeing flashes of black, white and chestnut as they rolled among the stems.

At last they rode clear in the sunlight with two little chicks between them—atoms of striped activity already water-wise. *(Fig. 50.)*

Dabchicks had no special haunts. They were liable to pop up any-where, often, like the hare, where least expected. The nests, small mounds of rotting flag and water-moss with a cup, almost awash, pressed in the top for eggs, were found in reeds, rushes, sedge and even floating amongst debris on open water.

They were not very easy to find. The sitting bird always covered the eggs by flicking loose bits over them before leaving the nest.

The nestling stripes on the young dabchicks' necks remained after they were as big as their parents. They often looked bigger than a parent hurrying towards them, wet from its dive, with food. *(Fig. 51.)* After a dabchick had been resting on the surface long enough to dry it seemed to wear more down than feathers.

Both waterhens and rails were found all over the fen in every kind of cover. Their long spreading toes let them climb about the undergrowth without troubling to consider the depth of water below it. Not that it mattered; they were both good swimmers although, unlike waterhens, the rails would not venture to cross open water if they could sneak round the side under cover.

But while waiting beside quiet pools I sometimes saw one paddle out from the border and swim across contentedly with the jerky action of a waterhen.

They were curious birds to watch at close range. The long red bill and thick outstretched neck were carried low as the rail hunted among the rushes. The short tail, often cocked over the back and half-hidden in its creamy coverts, and the short wings barely reaching beyond the slatted flank feathers, seemed to round off the bird prematurely. The legs, " knees " bent, looked as though they pivoted at a point behind the centre of gravity: the bird always seemed about to topple over. *(Fig. 52.)*

Their nests were well concealed, smaller and more compact than the openwork cradles of the waterhen.

This apparent overbalancing was also seen in herons as they crouched motionless with neck astretch and levelled, waiting for something to come within range of the bill. The long toes, spread to make a base to lever from, were not seen. The whole action of a heron was so rigidly controlled that it seemed as if the ragged body must conceal some clockwork mechanism rather than the vibrant muscles of a bird. *(Fig. 53.)*

In the spring of 1939 a heron got up from high reeds beside a flight-pool, sailed to the lode bank and stood watching me from there. The gulls, beginning to build nests in the pool, took no notice. They usually trailed after every passing heron and carrion crow, but this one wasn't mobbed at all.

I wondered then, and next week it happened again. She flew to the bank and presently came back and circled over the reeds. I let her circle half a dozen times to get my bearing, pushed in and found the nest.

It was built on a clump of giant sedge; a pile of reeds spattered with " whitewash," scales and residues of fish and filmy shafts of down. Two little herons, shock-headed Peters, nestled in the cup. They were about ten days old. *(Fig. 54.)*

I had found grey herons nesting on cliffs in Scotland and in reedbeds abroad, but those who used Adventurers Fen as a feeding ground came from a tree heronry six miles away. It was by no means overcrowded nor had they been felling trees. Is it possible that this bird was a Dutch one, exiled by the long, hard frost of the winter before?

Five herons of a smaller kind—cattle egrets, from Whipsnade—arrived in August 1937. They kept to the drier parts of the fen and stalked about

Fig. 55. Marsh Harrier after a Snipe

in surrounding fields for a few days, catching grasshoppers and flies.

Buzzards (common and rough-legged), peregrines, wild geese (pinkfoot and bean), paid occasional visits too in autumn, and marsh harriers, in time, might well have attempted to breed.

Most Aprils brought one or two of them to sail low over the fen on square, spread-finger-tipped wings. They were large and rather untidy compared to the other harriers. For all its buoyancy the flight hinted at the laboured flapping of a much heavier bird. But their bodies were light, almost as scrawny as a heron's, and they had long skinny yellow legs. When quartering they did not pounce as neatly as their relatives but stalled and made repeated clumsy grabs until they got, or lost, whatever they were after. *(Fig. 55.)*

By 1938 the fen was getting sadly overgrown with reeds above the waterline and Canadian weed below it. It was better in winter after the reeds had thinned and the weed had shrunk down: in summer their sheer exuberance drove out the diving birds and narrowed all open spaces.

But it favoured those birds whose interests centred on the reeds. The starlings in their tens of thousands, the hundreds of sand martins roosting by night; the reed warblers and chance wrens and blue tits foraging among the stems by day.

The reed warbler's whole life, summering in Europe, wintering in East Africa, is bounded by the reeds. Its colouring is theirs: russet above, ochre below, all softened by an overlying tinge of grey. It zig-zags chiding up the stems and flutters from them singing to totter down again with loose-knit wings and tail.

Fig. 56.
Sedge Warbler

This song-flight, the chatter, colour and all its actions were gentler and less extravagant than the sedge warbler's. Also the sedge warbler had a distinct eye-stripe and dark arrow-head markings down its back. (Fig. 56.) They were indifferent to reeds: I found them living in rank hedgerows miles from any water. Not so the reed warbler. A few might colonize osier beds and riverside tangles but they much preferred the reeds.

The nest is put in a thick cluster on the outskirts of a reedbed, along the margin of a pool or beside a water lane. There must be strong stems three or four years old to fix the framework to, although late nests may be built on stout green stems. The leaves around it must be grown to a sheaf some four feet high for concealment.

Strips of old flag sketch the cup and bind it to the stems; shreds and the fine stalks of the plumes pack and stiffen the walls; the feathery plumes themselves are used for lining. The nest is so deep and compact that the supporting reeds can be bent almost to water level without spilling the eggs—an insurance against wind.

In late seasons the nest is sometimes built in the niche of a reedmace stem. These offer protection earlier than reeds and poker-fluff may line the nest instead of reed plume. Moss and the fragile waterweed lying exposed at the base of the reeds are woven into late nests built over shallow water which afterwards recedes.

The cuckoo is the reed warbler's chief enemy. She sits by the hour on the high willows and nothing escapes her yellow eye. But a nest made to carry a fairy and four eggs for ten days and featherweight mites for eight days more won't always stand up to the wriggling of a fat young cuckoo for six weeks. With water all round there is

Fig. 57.
Reed Warbler

no alternative until his wings are competent and the nest may begin to slither slowly down its stems. I have found His Lordship sitting dangerously near the bottom on a pancaked nest.

A nest was accidentally overthrown while reed-cutting. It was reset by entwining its supporting reeds with those of a cluster standing a few yards away. Three eggs were fished up and replaced. The pair accepted our apology and a fortnight later three young reed warblers had hatched. It was amusing to watch the old birds sliding down the bannisters, a reed stem in each foot, to feed them. *(Fig. 57.)* The babies feathered and fledged and were expert at once in slithering about the reeds.

Perhaps it was the wealth of reeds that brought the bittern back in 1938. Its reappearance where it was familiar in the olden days seemed to set a hall mark on Adventurers Fen.

Bitterns had been recorded at odd times but none had nested for nearly a hundred years. Since February a bittern had been booming and I knew within a little the whereabouts of its nest. No search was made until June; by then the young should be fledged and no harm done by having a look at them. We found a nest in very dense reed but it was not the right one. There were four addled eggs and a fifth floating beside them. This one had an embryo inside it almost ready to hatch. There must have been a second nest not far away but we didn't prolong the search.

The old bittern threaded her way to the edge of the reed-bed. She rose and flew round croaking dismally, squinting at us down her Roman nose. *(Fig. 58.)* Her eyes looked forward like a gannet's, their gaze centering at a point just below the bill-tip. This gave her an odd expression but the focus was ideal for catching eels. She carried her neck more loosely than a heron and the beat of the wings was not so slow. Nor were the wings so broad: in spite of their pointed ends the flight was more suggestive of an owl's.

I often flushed the big, chequered bird from cover close beside me; it grunted and bowled silently away. Much less often I have been the vigilant and the bird off guard. Once, waiting for teal at dawn by a little pool, I had one fly right up to me. It turned aside and wavered slowly round the pool, looking from side to side. Twice it lowered its legs intending to pitch but, changing its mind, went on. The freckled buff and tawny striping of its plumage were those of the criss-cross shadows of the reeds.

The bittern is one of the few birds that would tempt me to spend hours in a hide: it's a forlorn hope to see much of it otherwise. But a good deal can be seen without limiting vision to a view-slit and missing all sorts of things happening outside.

*   *   *   *

ONE LAST LOOK ROUND

A hurried breakfast in the grey light before dawn: escape from the silent house to the cool, sweet air of early morning.

High Town drove, the fall in level along its straight three miles so slight that it could best be measured by the changing character of droveside hedge and ditch. Sloe and hawthorn first, then bramble, sallow and briar. Whitethroats purred and blackbirds hopped bemusedly along the path.

The boundary became more ditch than hedge: meadowsweet, comfrey, loosestrifes and the green spears and ragged top's'ls of reed invading the neglected grazing land on either side. Sedge warblers scolded and in the tangle of breast-high rankness a grasshopper warbler was reeling.

It was difficult to fix the origin exactly: I searched the scattered bushes where stems and grass-heads met for a slim, dark bird with a wedge tail.

It flew to the leader of a little bush and reeled on unafraid of my presence three yards off. Even so close, the sound faded as the head turned away and grew louder as it turned towards me. The inside of its beak was a translucent orange, the eyes fever bright as the slim body thrilled in ecstasy. I saw the hair-fine ticking on its cheeks and breast, the rich brown figuring on its back, faint wavy bands across the tail and the oat-shaped shadows round each eye. (*Fig. 59.*)

And then on to High Town bridge, the frontier: it was a point of honour to reach it before sunrise. A reed bunting sat on a stake cheeping and sleepily swinging his tail. He was huffy at being disturbed so early. (*Fig. 60.*)

A careful survey of the fen through glasses: there was the coot on her nest perched high in an island of sedges. She would remain a landmark till her eggs hatched out. Any new duck on the main sheet of water? Any new waders paddling round the edge?

Fig. 58. Bittern in Flight

Out of the south came five large waders flying high and calling: a double wader-whistle—bar-tailed godwits. They swept round in a wide half-circle and, descending, each bird wavered from the rest. One seemed to vote for this way, one for that. Agreed, they closed again and flew by leisurely, pitching a quarter-mile away. They sipped and rested from their journey, standing on one leg apiece with long bills tucked among the back feathers. *(Fig. 61.)*

As if overtired they couldn't settle comfortably: waders always fidget when they sleep. Later they rose and circled to gain height. They flew steadily north till my glasses could find them no longer.

Where were they bound? The Yenesi? Whence had they come? The Nile?

Fig. 59. *Grasshopper Warbler Reeling*

Fig. 60. *Cock Reed Bunting*

The track ran half-left up to Reach lode bank. You picked your way between dark green tufts of rush and the pale untidy hummocks of its fellow—jointed rush—whose nodes are almost imperceptible on the shining stems: they are better felt by running a stem through the fingers.

Half-way along a green sandpiper whistled shrilly and went winging away. Its white saddle gleamed as far as the eye could follow. *(Fig. 62.)*

Their custom was to zig-zag round in the sky on a five mile circle and drop back casually to the very puddle they left.

A few snipe, a family party of peewits, a garganey rose and settled farther from the track.

The waterlilies in Reach lode were opening, yellow and white in the weaving mist on the water. A pike lay grim in wait and motionless among the stems. Small fish played heedlessly about him: he had already fed.

There were more waders dabbling in the mud beside New Zealand. One, from its bulky foreparts, was a ruff: there was one redshank and the rest were reeves. The redshank's coral feet glinted in the sunlight unsoiled by the mud they ran upon. This ruff had orange legs and a sloe-black ruff and eartufts. His ladies' legs were grey or olive green; in one of them, almost yellow. Few birds vary so much in their colouring.

The redshank sprang up first, its yelping echoing across the fen. The others pattered along the edge a little while longer, then bunched together and took off. They flew loosely in echelon, lean, racy figures in silhouette. *(Fig. 63.)*

The trees beyond New Zealand were still heavy with mist. Cobwebs strung with dew linked thistle to thistle all along the bank. A wild duck flustered off. She sat uneasily in a little pool: her brood was hidden close at hand among the arrowheads and yellow flags.

Pout Hall, and a late flush of apple blossom on its forgotten orchard trees. A carrion crow was croaking from the top of a tall poplar on the Wicken side. They were the sentinels of the fen: you never set a foot inside its boundaries but what a carrion crow sat watching every step you took. They robbed the ducks and gulls and reed warblers of all the eggs and chicks they could discover. We shot as many as we could outwit and blew the bottoms out of their untidy nests, but still they came. It was a case of come back Peter, come back Paul.

A white shape flickered among the bushes in the angle between the lodes. It sailed into the open and began wavering towards me, but turned, and presently I saw it flop into the litter, stretching out a slim white-stockinged foot to take a vole. It was one of a pair of barn owls who have long made this far corner of the fen their own.

Seven o'clock—time for the owl, and for me too, to be making tracks for home.

Back along Burwell lode. A pheasant running on the bank ahead " cocked-up " and glided off into the fen. The sunshine glancing from the rigid wings seemed to set the bird afire. Some of the old litter stacks still stood, bindweed-covered mounds, but they had been there twenty years—a tribute to the lasting qualities of sedge. A kestrel flew from one of them with something in its claws.

Cockup Bridge: time and water had almost eaten through its lower timbers but it didn't shake when I climbed on its crooked back. Long ago a real "cock-up " bridge had stood there—a single weighted canti-lever arm which tipped-up to let the barges through and swung down again to let turf barrows cross the lode from one side of Adventurers Fen to the other (part of the Fen lay north of Burwell lode). And probably it will not be long before a third bridge supersedes the present one—of reinforced concrete, squat, incongruous and white.

The path turned right and led through heavy dew-soaked grasses to the fallen mill.

Swallows had glued their nest to a beam in one corner of its empty shell: there was a grey heron's feather peeping out. I climbed on the broken casing of the great slatted wheel to look inside—the wheel that had lifted untold tons of water in its time and sent it foamy-brown and hurrying along the deep Mill Drain behind. Four young swallows, nearly fledged, lay huddled in the nest with wisps of down still waving on their wide flat heads. Suddenly they all sat up. One of the parent swallows–the hen—skimmed through what was once a window, checked and hovered for a moment with a frill of insect legs and wings all round her bill, and fled. She seemed more surprised than worried to find me standing there. I stepped aside. She glided in again, went straight to the nest, fed two of her brood and went out without a twitter of resentment at my trespassing.

Beyond the mill the path led past a grassy field where a pair of yellow wagtails, perched on thistle heads a hundred yards apart, were anxiously flirting their tails. They had four eggs hidden in a tuft.

And so to the old pump sleeping under its willows at the head of the ten foot drain.

The sun slanted on the still brown water. It was yeasty with very small life, cyclops, daphnia and still smaller forms. Inch-long fishes darted among the swarms and gobbled greedily. A waterbeetle rowed up from the depths and hung for a moment on the surface upsidedown to breathe. It got a fish and went back again, carrying it in jagged shiny jaws. A little pike dashed out and took another one: there was a glittering flash and the pike itself was gone. A kingfisher sat on the railing above holding it in its beak. It smacked the pike repeatedly against the rail and gulped it down. *(Fig. 64.)* There was no smirk of satisfaction, the kingfisher took it all as a matter of course.

We watched each other, the kingfisher on its broken rail, I leaning in the dapple of the willows against the pump, only the ten foot drain between us. I was there first: it had not seen me come and even now was half inclined to doubt if that still figure, with the grey and gold of leaf and sunfleck dancing over it, could really be a man. I made no movement to enlighten it. It wanted to rest, to let the little pike digest, but dared not do so with that query unsolved under the willow opposite. It kept turning its head from side to side, peering this way and that, bobbing up and down and flicking its stumpy little tail, cheeping each time it did it. For a little while now and then it relaxed, only to grow uneasy and start fussing all over again. We watched each other for a good ten minutes.

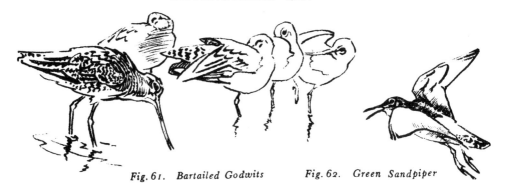

Fig. 61.   *Bartailed Godwits*   Fig. 62.   *Green Sandpiper*

For all the glitter of its jewellery the kingfisher was not a prepossessing bird.   The squat body, exquisite in colouring, had neither neck nor crupper to fine it down.   The small vermilion toes were impotent to off-set the heavy bill and, above all, the bird had a cold, expressionless stare.

Fig. 63.   *Ruff, Reeves and Redshank in Flight*

66

It would not worry overmuch to find its living gone, the pools dried out, the fen laid bare. There are little fish and broken rails to sit on in plenty of other places. It must be so. Nature cannot let sentiment usurp her laws: that is for us to feel. Adventurers Fen in all its loveliness has gone but nature goes on elsewhere.

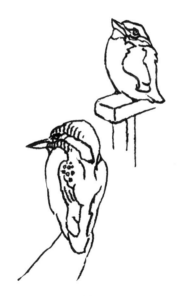

Fig. 64.
Kingfishers

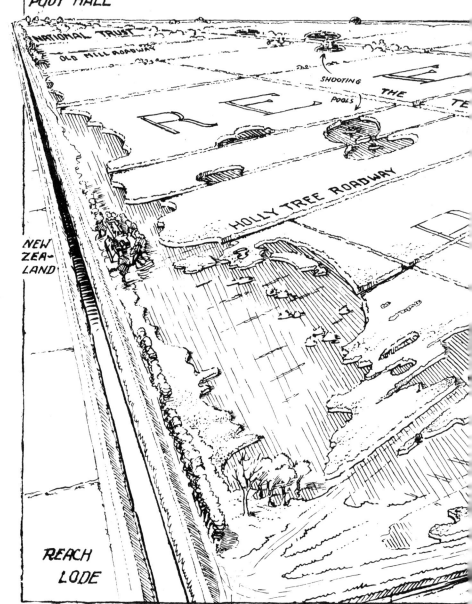

DIAGRAM (B) of ADVENTURERS FEN
~ the whole area, reed beds, roadways, e
POUT HALL

NATIONAL TRUST
OLD MILL ROADWAY
SHOOTING
POOLS
THE
RE E
HOLLY TREE ROADWAY
NEW
ZEA-
LAND
REACH
LODE